STUART PATERSON

Stuart Paterson's children's plays, first performed at Glasgow's Citizen's Theatre, Edinburgh's Royal Lyceum, Dundee Repertory Theatre and Newcastle Playhouse, have since been staged throughout the UK. They include *Merlin The Magnificent*, *The Snow Queen*, *Beauty and the Beast*, *Cinderella*, *Granny and the Gorilla*, *The Princess and the Goblin*, *The Sleeping Beauty*, a one-act play *The Secret Voice*, and an adaptation of Roald Dahl's *George's Marvellous Medicine*. In 1998 *Hansel and Gretel* was nominated for the Barclays Best Children's Production of the Year Award.

He has written *King of the Fields* for the Traverse Theatre and new versions of Chekhov's *The Cherry Orchard* and *Uncle Vanya*. For The Scottish Youth Theatre he has written *In Traction* (later televised by BBC) and adapted Zola's *Germinal*. He has also adapted Zola's *Therese Raquin* for Communicado Theatre Company, which was also staged at Newcastle Playhouse and Edinburgh's Royal Lyceum. His work for Tag Theatre Company includes an adaptation of James Hogg's *The Private Memoirs and Confessions of a Justified Sinner*, and a new version of J. M. Barrie's *Peter Pan* staged at the Royal Lyceum, Edinburgh. He has recently completed a new version of *Comrades* by August Strindberg for the Royal Lyceum and an adaptation of *The Ballroom of Romance* by William Trevor for Northern Stage.

His television credits include *The Old Course* (BBC) and the film *Workhorses*, which won The Pharic Mclaren Award.

His short film *Somebody's Wee Nobody* won the Gold Award at the Chicago International Film Festival. Current film projects include original screenplays *The Pretender*, *Whisky Mac*, *Under the Same Moon*, *The Chieftain's Daughter* and screen adaptations of *The Kelpie's Pearls* by Mollie Hunter, *Fergus Lanont* by Robin Jenkins and Shusaku Edo's *Scandal*.

STUART PATERSON

Cinderella

with an Afterword by the author

NICK HERN BOOKS

London

www.nickhernbooks.co.uk

A Nick Hern Book

Cinderella first published in Great Britain in 2000
as an original paperback by Nick Hern Books Limited,
14 Larden Road, London W3 7ST

Cinderella © 2000 by Stuart Paterson

Stuart Paterson has asserted his right to be identified as
the author of this work

Front cover illustration by Lauren Hamill,
Class P2 from Lauder Primary School

Typeset by Country Setting, Kingsdown, Kent CT14 8ES
Printed and bound in Great Britain by Biddles, Guildford

A CIP catalogue record for this book is available from
the British Library

ISBN 185459 4842

To Joan, Alana, Patrick and Bruno
with love and thanks

Cinderella was first performed at the Royal Lyceum Theatre, Edinburgh, on 5 December 1989, with the following cast:

ISABELLA/CINDERELLA	Karen Westwood
CLAUDIA/ FAIRY GODMOTHER	Victoria Hardcastle
FATHER	Iain Agnew
CLAUDINE	Nicola Grier
CLAUDETTE	Andrea Hart
SERGEANT PUFF	Billy McElhaney
CALLUM/DANCING BEAR	Iain Andrew
BLACK DOUGLAS/KING JOHN	James Bryce
PRINCE RUFUS	Robin Sneller

Extras Edward Cory, Stella Craven, Martin Donahue, David Roylance

Musicians Savourna Stevenson, Ronnie Goodman, John Kenny

Director Hugh Hodgart
Designer Gregory Smith
Lighting Designer Kevin Sleep
Composer/MD Savourna Stevenson
Movement/Choreography Rita Henderson

Note: *Cinderella was first written for a cast of nine or more, the version printed here can be performed by eight or more.*

Characters

CINDERELLA / ISABELLA
CLAUDIA
FATHER
CALLUM
CLAUDINE
CLAUDETTE
PUFF
BOY
FAIRY GODMOTHER
KING
PRINCE
KITCHEN WORKERS
GUESTS
GUARD
THE BLACK DOUGLAS
DANCING BEAR

Possible doubling for a cast of eight:

CLAUDIA / FAIRY GODMOTHER
CALLUM / DANCING BEAR
THE BLACK DOUGLAS / PRINCE
FATHER / KING

Other doublings are possible.

Music

A tape of music to accompany the play, used in several previous productions, is available for hire. For more information please contact Nick Hern Books, The Glasshouse, 49a Goldhawk Road, London W12 8QP. Companies should also feel free to use their own music.

ACT ONE

Scene One

Music. The castle gates, from inside the castle grounds. A silver birch tree, like a slender young girl, grows by a simple grave.

Enter ISABELLA, *furtively. A voice calls out.*

VOICE (*angrily, from off*). Isabella! Where are you, Isabella?

ISABELLA *hides.*

Enter CLAUDIA – *a stern and forbidding figure with her hair covered and her dark clothes.*

CLAUDIA. How dare you run away from me! (*Looks around, fails to see* ISABELLA.) Show yourself! This minute! Isabella, where are you?

She exits.

ISABELLA *comes out of hiding.*

ISABELLA (*quietly, after* CLAUDIA). Leave me alone! I'll come here if I want to.

She kneels by the grave, remembers.

Enter CLAUDIA. *She watches, unseen by* ISABELLA.

ISABELLA.
Moon light
Moon bright
New moon
Seen tonight
I wish I may
I wish I might
Have the wish
I wish tonight.

CLAUDIA. Isabella!

ISABELLA *starts, looks around fearfully, hopefully, then sees* CLAUDIA.

ISABELLA (*disappointed*). It's you, Claudia.

CLAUDIA. Who did you think it was?

ISABELLA. My . . . mother said that to me every night –
Moon light, Moon bright . . . Then she would kiss me and I
would fall asleep.

CLAUDIA. I've been looking everywhere for you!

ISABELLA. Well now you've found me. (*Waves cheekily.*)
Bye-bye.

CLAUDIA (*a flash of cold fury*). I could murder . . . !
(*Controls herself.*) The Lord-General, your father, expects
me to look after you. Come inside . . . It's cold.

ISABELLA. I'll stay . . . I'm never cold here.

CLAUDIA. I told you to stay away from this place! Always
running to your mother's grave – she's gone and she'll
never come back! (*Strokes* ISABELLA's *hair.*) Now you
have others who care for you . . . Come inside.

ISABELLA *pulls away, goes to the tree.*

ISABELLA (*half under her breath*). You're stupid!

CLAUDIA. I beg your pardon!

ISABELLA. My mother is dead, I know that, but I still
remember what she said to me on the night she died . . .
She said . . .

CLAUDIA (*with massive authority*). You're too young to talk
about such things!

ISABELLA. She smiled and she took my hand and she said –
'I think of my body as my reflection . . . When I die I'll
leave it behind because I won't need it anymore . . . But the
real me won't die . . . The real me won't die.'

CLAUDIA (*impatiently*). Never heard such nonsense!

ISABELLA. You see – you are stupid.

CLAUDIA. I've just about had enough of your . . . (*Controls
her evil temper, self-pityingly.*) So this is all the thanks

I get. (*Tearfully.*) After all I've done for you, after all my kindness . . .

ISABELLA (*taken in*). Don't cry, Claudia.

CLAUDIA. I'll go! I know when I'm not wanted. (*Goes to exit.*)

ISABELLA. No, don't go . . . Please stay. (CLAUDIA *stays.*) You have been kind – in your own way. I'm sorry . . . I'll do anything I can to make it up to you.

CLAUDIA (*suddenly full of hungry life*). Anything, did you say?

ISABELLA (*taken aback*). Y-yes.

CLAUDIA. Very well. I want you to talk to your father – on my behalf.

ISABELLA. My father . . . On your . . . You mean . . . ?

CLAUDIA. Yes – I wish to marry your father.

ISABELLA (*shocked*). Marry him! You must ask him yourself.

CLAUDIA. Oh, we have talked about it many times.

ISABELLA. I didn't know that!

CLAUDIA. But he needs your blessing. You know he thinks only of you.

ISABELLA. Yes, but . . .

CLAUDIA. He'll never be lonely again . . . And you know how much I . . . love you.

ISABELLA. It's true – he is lonely.

CLAUDIA. Then you will speak to him.

ISABELLA *nods her agreement.*

CLAUDIA. Good girl! (*Kisses* ISABELLA.) I'll be like a new mother to you – you'll see.

ISABELLA. Here comes my father.

CLAUDIA. Your father! Quickly, you must be alone with him. (*Urgently.*) Don't let me down! (*Goes to exit.*)

ISABELLA. Wait . . .

CLAUDIA. I'm relying on you!

CLAUDIA *hides.*

ISABELLA (*to* AUDIENCE, *simply*). Why can't they ever just leave you alone?

Enter The Lord-General, ISABELLA'S FATHER.

FATHER. There's my little girl. You mustn't come here so much. (*Puts his arm around her.*) I miss her too, but life goes on . . . We must not be sad.

ISABELLA. I'm not, father.

FATHER. Good girl . . . But look at your tree.

ISABELLA. It's grown and grown.

FATHER. It was clever of you to plant it . . . It's far more beautiful than a lump of stone.

ISABELLA. Father . . . I was wondering . . .

FATHER. What were you wondering?

ISABELLA. Oh I wonder lots of things . . . I wonder what will ever become of me, and I wonder why all your soldiers are scared of you when I'm not scared of you at all, and I wonder . . .

FATHER (*laughing*). What a lot of big thoughts for such a little girl.

ISABELLA. . . . And I wonder what it would be like if you married Claudia.

FATHER. Married Claudia! How did you . . . What put that idea in your head?

ISABELLA. She's plain and she's good, and you wouldn't be sad or lonely any more.

FATHER. It's true, and it's high time you had a new mother! But I'll do nothing against your wishes, I promise you that. Tell me, Isabella – would it make you happy if I married Claudia?

ISABELLA. If it makes you happy it will make me happy.

FATHER. Then it's settled! I'll ask her first thing in the morning. Come inside . . . I'll marry her and we'll all be happy together . . . Come on, now.

Exeunt FATHER *and* ISABELLA.

CLAUDIA *emerges from hiding, her eyes blazing with joy and triumph.*

CLAUDIA. I can't breathe, I can't keep still. The joy, the joy! (*Stamps her foot to earth her excitement.*) She has played into my hands. Her father will be mine, the castle will be mine, all I ever remember wanting – mine, mine! And as for Little Miss Moonlight! (*Mimics* ISABELLA.) 'If it makes you happy it will make me happy.' Yeeeuurk! She makes me want to be sick. I'd like to smack her ears with a stick! What was it she said about me? (*Mimics* ISABELLA.) 'She's plain and she's good.' We'll see about that, my little pet. (*Uncovers her head and shakes loose her fiery red hair.*) I've always hated her, but I've had to hide it. NO MORE HIDING! Oh yes, I'll teach her a lesson! (*To* AUDIENCE.) And there's nothing you can do to stop me. I don't care what you think because ALL CHILDREN ARE STUPID LITTLE BRATS! (*Stamps her foot.*) OH YES YOU ARE! You can shout all you like – it just makes ignoring you all the more enjoyable . . . And so my little Isabella, I give you my word, by my bones and my blood, I hate you and I will make your life a misery. Watch me now!

Stamps her foot. Blackout.

Scene Two

The main hall of ISABELLA'S FATHER's *castle.*

Loud, angry shouts from off.

Enter ISABELLA *at a run, carrying a piece of cake.*

Enter CLAUDINE *and* CLAUDETTE, CLAUDIA's *daughters – chasing* ISABELLA.

CLAUDINE. Give me, give me, give me!

CLAUDETTE. Want it, want it, want it!

ISABELLA. This is mine! You're not getting it.

CLAUDINE (*wheedling*). Please, Isabella – we are your new sisters.

ISABELLA. I've told you – no.

CLAUDINE *and* CLAUDETTE (*in unison*). BUT WE LOVE CAKE!

ISABELLA. You've already had twice as much as me.

CLAUDINE. Our mother always gives us twice as much.

CLAUDETTE. Because she loves us twice as much as you.

ISABELLA. Leave me alone.

CLAUDETTE. You're forgetting, Isabella.

CLAUDINE. We're older than you.

CLAUDETTE. We're bigger.

CLAUDINE *and* CLAUDETTE (*in unison*). AND WE'RE BETTER!

CLAUDINE. So give us the cake.

ISABELLA. No – it's mine.

CLAUDETTE. Then we'll just have to take it!

ISABELLA (*fiercely*). Come on, then! Take it – come on! (CLAUDINE *and* CLAUDETTE *do nothing.*) I didn't think so. (CLAUDINE *makes a move,* ISABELLA *eludes her.*) LAY A FINGER ON MY PIECE OF CAKE AND I'LL RATTLE YOUR TEETH! (*With quiet menace.*) I mean it.

CLAUDINE (*backing off*). She's horrible, Claudette.

CLAUDETTE. So she is, Claudine. She always saves her bit just so she's still got hers when we've eaten ours all up!

ISABELLA. You can't control yourself, that's all. You're greedy.

CLAUDINE (*huffed*). You can keep your cake.

CLAUDETTE (*huffed*). We don't want it anymore.

ISABELLA. Good! I'm going to try on my dress for the royal ball – so I'll leave my cake here. (*Puts cake down,* CLAUDINE *and* CLAUDETTE *follow it greedily with their eyes*.) And I'm warning you – it had better be here when I get back!

CLAUDINE *and* CLAUDETTE (*in unison*). We're not greedy pigs!

ISABELLA. Or else!

She exits.

CLAUDETTE. Huh, I couldn't care less about her smelly piece of cake.

CLAUDINE. Neither could I, Claudette.

CLAUDETTE. Oh but I do care, Claudine. I'd kill for cake!

CLAUDINE. So would I! You take the first bite.

CLAUDETTE. No – you go first.

CLAUDINE (*reaches for cake, pulls back*). I can't! I'm scared of Isabella.

CLAUDETTE. So am I, Claudine. She's stronger than she looks.

CLAUDINE. This is horrible. I really want her cake, it's right in front of my nose, and I can't have it!

CLAUDINE *and* CLAUDETTE (*in unison, stamping and wailing*). It's not fair! It's not fair!

Enter CLAUDIA, *now beautifully dressed as befits the lady of the castle.*

CLAUDIA. My little treasures . . . There, there, tell mother what the matter is.

CLAUDETTE. Isabella won't give us her cake.

CLAUDINE. She got so angry she nearly hit us.

CLAUDIA. My poor lambs.

CLAUDETTE. It's not your fault, mama.

CLAUDINE. We're glad you married again and brought us here. Who ever thought we'd live in a castle? Everything's lovely.

CLAUDETTE. Except for Isabella!

CLAUDINE. You promised to get rid of her – and she's still here.

CLAUDETTE (*shivers*). I hate her!

CLAUDINE. She thinks she's better than us.

CLAUDETTE. Yes, and even when we say really cruel things to her she just puts her hands over her ears and whistles.

CLAUDINE. And anyway we want her bedroom!

CLAUDETTE. It's got the best view, and a huge mirror on the wall.

CLAUDINE. But the worst thing is everyone likes her better than us.

CLAUDETTE (*indicates* AUDIENCE). Even they like her better than us.

CLAUDIA. But they hardly know you.

CLAUDINE. It doesn't matter. We can tell.

CLAUDIA. Then that means they're every bit as stupid and horrible as Isabella! NEVER FORGET – YOU ARE BETTER THAN ISABELLA AND (*Indicates* AUDIENCE.) YOU ARE BETTER THAN THEM! (*To* AUDIENCE.) Smelly, revolting little brats! Oh yes you are!

AUDIENCE. Oh no we're not!

ALL. Oh yes you are!

AUDIENCE. Oh no we're not!

CLAUDIA (*to her daughters*). You have my permission to ignore them completely!

CLAUDINE *and* CLAUDETTE
(*chanting in unison, to* AUDIENCE).
We don't care what you think!
We don't care what you think!
We're OK and you stink!
We're OK and you stink!

CLAUDINE. Oh but mama, please can we get rid of Isabella?

CLAUDETTE. Please can we?

CLAUDINE *and* CLAUDETTE (*in unison*). Please, please, please, please, please, please, please, please!

CLAUDIA. Oh yes we'll get rid of her, my treasures. We'll make her wish she'd never been born!

CLAUDETTE. I love you, mama.

CLAUDIA. But we have to hurry. There are only three days until the royal ball . . . She must not be allowed to go.

CLAUDINE. How can we stop her?

CLAUDIA. First we must make her look bad in front of her father.

CLAUDINE. Brilliant!

CLAUDETTE. She'll hate that more than anything!

CLAUDINE (*excited, perplexed*). But how?

CLAUDIA (*with chilling assurance*). Come to mother and she will tell you.

They form a secretive huddle. The sound of horrid whisperings and evil laughter.

CLAUDINE (*looking up*). She's coming!

CLAUDIA (*urgently*). Claudette, stand by the cake – quickly! Claudine, keep watch for him.

Enter ISABELLA *wearing a simple red dress.*

ISABELLA (*to* CLAUDINE). What are you looking so pleased about?

CLAUDINE. None of your business.

ISABELLA (*to* CLAUDIA). So you're here too.

CLAUDIA. You? You? I've told you, Isabella – you may call me Lady Claudia or you may call me Mother.

ISABELLA (*quietly, hardly daring it*). You'll be lucky!

CLAUDIA. What did you say!

ISABELLA. I said . . . nothing.

CLAUDIA. Just as well for you! (*Loudly, mockingly, straight to her face.*) And where did you get that stupid dress?

ISABELLA. It's not stupid . . . My mother made it for me . . . I'm going to wear it to the royal ball.

CLAUDIA. You'll wear what I tell you to wear!

ISABELLA. I'll wear what I like.

CLAUDIA. Then I won't let you go!

ISABELLA. Try and stop me!

CLAUDIA. Just you listen to me, my girl!

ISABELLA. Why should I? You're a liar.

CLAUDIA. How dare you!

ISABELLA. It's true . . . You say you love me and anyone can see that's a lie . . . And when you married my father I didn't know about . . . about them. (*Indicates* CLAUDINE *and* CLAUDETTE.) You never told me they would be coming too.

CLAUDINE *and* CLAUDETTE (*in unison, outraged*). Huh!

CLAUDIA (*childishly, mockingly*). Oh did poor little Isabella want to be the only one, did she want to be the only little girl? (*Suddenly hard and fierce.*) WELL LET ME TELL YOU THERE ARE OTHER PEOPLE IN THE WORLD EVERY BIT AS IMPORTANT AS YOU! AND IF YOU THINK I'M GOING TO PUT UP WITH YOUR INSOLENCE ONE SECOND LONGER YOU'VE GOT ANOTHER THING COMING! YOU'VE MET YOUR MATCH IN ME, MY GIRL, MAKE NO MISTAKE ABOUT THAT!

CLAUDETTE (*delighted*). Oh I love this.

CLAUDIA (*relentless*). I'M GOING TO PUT A STOP TO YOUR NONSENSE! BY THE TIME I'VE FINISHED WITH YOU THEY'LL NEED A CLOTH TO WIPE YOU OFF THE FLOOR!

CLAUDINE *and* CLAUDETTE *clap, dance with joy.*

ISABELLA. Why are you always shouting at me?

CLAUDINE *and* CLAUDETTE (*in unison*). Tell her, mama!

CLAUDIA. I'M ALWAYS SHOUTING AT YOU BECAUSE
EVERY TIME I SEE YOU YOU'RE DOING
SOMETHING THAT MAKES MY BLOOD BOIL! DO
YOU THINK I ENJOY SHOUTING AT YOU?
(ISABELLA *puts her hands over her ears and whistles.*)
ANSWER ME THAT, MY GIRL! THERE ARE A
HUNDRED THINGS I COULD BE DOING RATHER
THAN STANDING HERE SHOUTING AT YOU!

ISABELLA. I'm not listening. (*Whistles.*)

CLAUDIA. I'M NOT FINISHED WITH YOU! YOU ARE A
STUPID AND SELFISH LITTLE GIRL! YOU'RE LAZY
AND MESSY AND YOU THINK ABOUT NOBODY
EXCEPT FOR YOURSELF!

ISABELLA (*her hands still over her ears*). Can't hear you.

CLAUDINE (*looking off*). He's coming!

CLAUDIA. AND NOW I'M GOING TO TEACH YOU A
LESSON YOU'LL NEVER FORGET! Claudette, eat her
cake.

CLAUDETTE *guzzles the cake, gives a piece to*
CLAUDINE. *They make a great show of enjoying it.*

ISABELLA. Still can't hear you . . . (*Sees* CLAUDINE *and*
CLAUDETTE *eating her cake.*) That's mine. You can't do
that. That's mine!

She hurls herself at CLAUDINE *in a blind rage, shakes her
violently, pushes her to the floor and continues her attack.*

CLAUDINE. Help! She's killing me!

ISABELLA (*strangling her*). It's mine. Spit it out. It's mine!

Enter FATHER.

FATHER. What's going on? Isabella – stop that! (ISABELLA
continues her assault.) I said – stop it!

He pulls ISABELLA *away from* CLAUDINE.

ISABELLA. I warned them!

CLAUDINE (*in a croaky voice*). She's a wild animal!

CLAUDIA (*to* FATHER). Now do you believe me? She's like this all the time.

ISABELLA. That's not true!

FATHER. I would never have believed it of you, Isabella.

CLAUDIA (*to* FATHER) Oh yes, she's as good as gold when you're here – but as soon as your back's turned she's a different girl.

ISABELLA (*desperately, to herself*). I'll go mad.

FATHER. DON'T INTERRUPT!

CLAUDIA. The girl's wild, she's completely out of control. She can't be allowed to go on like this. (*Tearfully.*) I'm at my wit's end.

FATHER (*embracing her*). There, there now.

CLAUDIA (*tearfully*). I love her so much.

FATHER. I know you do.

ISABELLA. I will go mad.

FATHER. KEEP QUIET, ISABELLA!

ISABELLA. But . . .

FATHER. DO WHAT YOU'RE TOLD! (ISABELLA, *hurt, hangs her head.*) If, Isabella, if you promise to be a good girl from now on, I'm sure we'll all forgive you.

CLAUDINE *and* CLAUDETTE *look worried that* ISABELLA *will go unpunished.* CLAUDIA *tries to silence them with a quick gesture, unseen by* FATHER.

CLAUDINE *and* CLAUDETTE (*huffed, in unison*). Huh!

FATHER. But I'm going to market today. I'll bring you all presents.

CLAUDETTE. What kind of presents?

FATHER. You tell me.

CLAUDETTE. Diamonds and rubies?

FATHER. Yes.

CLAUDINE. Cream croquettes?

CLAUDETTE. Chocolate squeezers?

FATHER. Of course.

CLAUDINE. And silk dresses?

FATHER. Only the very best.

CLAUDETTE (*kissing him*). We love you.

CLAUDINE (*kissing him*). You're the best Daddy in the whole world.

FATHER. And you, Isabella – what would you like?

ISABELLA. Nothing.

FATHER (*angered again*). Ask for nothing and nothing is all you'll get! I'll try again . . . What would you like?

ISABELLA. I would like a branch from the tree growing beside my mother's grave.

CLAUDIA (*seizing her chance*). Do you see, do you see what I have to put up with?

FATHER. Why can't she be like everybody else?

ISABELLA. I don't want to be like everybody else!

CLAUDIA (*gently, schemingly*). Everything will be alright, my dear little Isabella – you'll see. (*Puts her arm around her.*) I'm sure one day you'll love me every bit as much as your real mother.

ISABELLA (*pulling away*). No!

FATHER. Mind your manners!

ISABELLA. I'll never love you! I hate you!

CLAUDIA (*triumphant*). There you are! Now you see what she's really like! THE GIRL MUST BE PUNISHED!

ISABELLA. Do what you like – I don't care!

FATHER (*furious*). OH YOU'LL CARE, MY GIRL – DON'T YOU WORRY!

CLAUDETTE (*winks at* CLAUDIA). She's got the manners of a kitchen girl.

CLAUDIA (*winks back*). What a good idea, Claudette. Since she's only got the manners of a kitchen girl – IT'S TO THE KITCHEN SHE MUST GO!

ISABELLA (*surprised, frightened*). Please, no – don't send me there.

CLAUDIA. Yes, yes! You will live and work in the kitchen until you learn your lesson. There's no more royal ball for you!

ISABELLA. You planned this!

CLAUDINE *and* CLAUDETTE (*in unison*). To the kitchen, to the kitchen, to the kitchen!

CLAUDIA (*clapping her hands sternly*). Quiet girls – your father is thinking.

FATHER. I've made up my mind.

ISABELLA. Father? Please, father . . .

FATHER (*thunderous*). TO THE KITCHEN WITH HER!

ISABELLA *exits, defeated.* CLAUDIA *approaches* FATHER, *strokes his arm.*

CLAUDIA. Don't blame yourself, dear husband . . . It had to be done . . . It's for the best . . .

FATHER *nods sadly, and exits.* CLAUDIA *and her daughters wait until they are sure he is gone before celebrating their victory with horrid glee – shouting, clapping, dancing with joy.*

CLAUDIA. Come, my treasures, and let us enjoy our new life . . . Everything is ours, and nothing is hers!

Exeunt.

Scene Three

The castle kitchen. A terrifying and exciting place of hard, relentless work. Vast, shadowy, practical. A beautiful old hearth. Huge ovens glow and flare. Giant pots release jets of steam. The only window is high up and heavily barred.

KITCHEN WORKERS *toil in the heat from the ovens.* SERGEANT PUFF, *the castle cook, moves among them, bullying, fussing, barking instructions.*

PUFF. Hurry, hurry!
    Stir the soup, scrub the floor
    That goes there, behind the door
    Hurry, hurry!
    Move yourself, don't tell me you're tired
    Salt in that water, more wood on the fire
    Hurry, hurry!
    Heads down, don't let that fall
    We've got to make the food for the royal ball
    Hurry, hurry!
    The day's nearly over, don't dare answer back
    Turn the chicken, tie up that sack
    Hurry, hurry!

Only the KITCHEN BOY, *working hard and quickly, escapes* PUFF's *criticism. He is wild-looking, his features almost obscured by his unkempt hair and the dirt on his face.*

Enter ISABELLA *struggling with a heavy sack. Her dress has been turned to rags by hard work.*

PUFF. Come on, girl – come on! (*Despite her best efforts she lets the sack fall.*) Take a shake to yourself, girl! You'll have to do better than that (*But the* BOY *has lifted the sack, stowed it, and commenced another task before* ISABELLA *can even say thank you.*) And don't think there'll always be someone else to do your work for you. Here! (*Throws her a broom, she catches it.*) Make yourself useful. (ISABELLA *commences to sweep the floor.*) Put your back into it!

ISABELLA (*wearily*). I'm trying my best.

PUFF. Then your best ain't good enough! Try harder! (*She*

tries harder.) Keep going, men – the day's only done when the work's been done! Keep going or I'll feed you to The Black Douglas! (*The* KITCHEN WORKERS *hurry to lay out the food for the ball, tidy up at the end of the day.* ISABELLA *tries to keep up with the frantic, skilled pace of the work, but she succeeds only in getting in the way.*) Look where you're going, girl! You've been here long enough to know better!

ISABELLA (*angrily, throwing down her broom*). I've told you – I'm trying my best! (*Silence.* ISABELLA *is near to tears.*) Don't shout at me . . . Please don't shout . . .

PUFF (*seeing how near tears are*). That's enough for today, boys. You've made food fit for a King. Away you go and have a cup of tea. You've earned it. (*The* WORKERS, *weary and a little embarrassed, leave the kitchen. The* BOY *stays, watching* ISABELLA. PUFF *picks up the broom, hands it to her, speaks kindly.*) Here . . . Here's your brush.

ISABELLA (*taking it, quietly*). Thank you.

PUFF. Good girl . . . I'm sorry for shouting . . . It's not just you, though. I shout at everybody. (*To* BOY.) Isn't that right? I used to shout at you a hundred times every day and now I don't have to shout any more. (BOY *nods and smiles.*) I take everything very seriously! (*Begins to pace, shout, wag his finger, shake his fist.*) There's nothing I hate more than seeing a job badly done! (BOY *imitates* PUFF *behind his back.*) I've been in kitchens where nobody did a thing they were told! Everybody just stood about laughing – AND NOTHING EVER GOT DONE! WELL, IT WON'T BE LIKE THAT IN MY KITCHEN! NO, SIR – NOT IN THE KITCHEN OF SERGEANT PUFF! I HAVE NEVER DISOBEYED AN ORDER AND I HAVE NEVER LAUGHED!

ISABELLA (*amused at* BOY*'s imitation*). You've never done something you were told not to?

PUFF (*proudly*). Not once.

ISABELLA (*fighting against laughter*). But you must have laughed.

PUFF. I have never laughed. (*To* BOY.) Have you ever seen me
   laugh?

   BOY *shakes his head.*

ISABELLA. Never ever?

PUFF. Never ever!

ISABELLA. Why not?

   BOY *imitates* PUFF *again, behind his back.*

PUFF (*annoyed at the laughter shining in her eyes*). I'LL
   TELL YOU WHY NOT! BECAUSE LIFE IS NO
   LAUGHING-MATTER, THAT'S WHY NOT! (ISABELLA
   laughs openly. PUFF *turns around, catches the* BOY *imitating him, chases him.*) I'll kick you up in the air, you cheeky
   little monkey! (*Gives up chase.*) I'd laugh if I could . . . I've
   tried and I've tried, I just can't do it.

ISABELLA. I wasn't laughing at you.

PUFF. I don't mind others laughing, as long as they get on
   with their work! (*Indicates* BOY.) He's a good worker. You
   should try to be more like him.

ISABELLA. Like him? No thank you.

PUFF. And why not?

ISABELLA. He never says a word, and, well . . . he's filthy
   dirty.

PUFF. He can speak when he wants and he's only dirty
   because he does all the hardest work . . . So listen to me –
   if you try harder at your work, I'll try not to shout so much.
   Is it a bargain? (ISABELLA *nods.*) Then we'll be great
   pals. (*Offers her his hand, they shake on it.*) Good girl.
   I'm away for my dinner – chicken beak soup, and pig's tail
   stew . . . There's plenty if you want it.

   He exits.

   The BOY *sits in a corner.*

ISABELLA (*tentatively*). I'm not hungry . . . Are you hungry?
   (BOY *produces a lump of bread from his clothing, bites into
   it.*) Thanks for helping me. (BOY *shrugs.*) What's your

name? Won't you tell me? (BOY *shrugs*.) I didn't mean to be rude when I said you were dirty . . . I'm not used to work – and that man! Imagine never laughing in your whole life . . . Isn't that the funniest thing you've ever heard? (BOY *shrugs*.) My name's Isabella, in case you wanted to know. (BOY *shrugs*.) Is that all you can do? (*She imitates his shrug*.) Well, is it? (BOY s*hrugs*.) Suit yourself – you don't have to talk if you don't . . .

BOY. You were nearly crying.

ISABELLA. I was not nearly crying!

BOY. You were, I saw you. You've got to be strong to work in the kitchen.

ISABELLA (*shivers*). It's so dark down here, and at night when I sleep on the floor the fire makes shapes on the walls.

BOY. There are demons in the ovens, and ghosts in the chimney.

ISABELLA. Don't say that!

BOY. You've got to be strong.

ISABELLA. I am strong . . . Only tonight's the night of the royal ball . . . I've never wanted to go to anything so much in all my life – and now I can't go . . . I hate this kitchen.

BOY (*dismissively*). Three days you've been here.

ISABELLA. It feels like forever.

BOY. I've been here for three years.

ISABELLA. Three years! That is forever.

BOY. But one day I'll escape from here.

ISABELLA. Escape? Are you a prisoner here too?

BOY. Why else would I be in this place?

ISABELLA. Where will you go when you escape?

BOY. To my home, far beyond The Northern Mountains.

ISABELLA. That sounds wonderful . . . But the castle walls are so high and the mountains so far away. Will you ever get there? (*He gives no answer*.) I hope you do.

The BOY *breaks off a piece of bread, offers it to*
ISABELLA.

BOY. Here. (*She accepts the bread, eats it.*) The food down
here is horrible.

ISABELLA. I know – chicken beak soup!

BOY. All the good food is sent upstairs . . . Look. (*Takes the
cloth off the trays of food for the royal ball.*) When I think
of all they get I want to spit in their food.

ISABELLA. You wouldn't dare.

BOY. Wouldn't I? Watch.

He makes to spit.

ISABELLA. Don't!

BOY. Why not?

ISABELLA. It's revolting!

BOY. One of these days I'll do it . . . You get everything you
want up there.

ISABELLA. That's what you think.

A horrid babbling is heard from off.

BOY. What's that noise?

ISABELLA. Oh no – now you'll see what it's really like up
there.

Enter CLAUDINE *and* CLAUDETTE, *dressed for the royal
ball, giving themselves ridiculous airs.*

CLAUDINE *and* CLAUDETTE (*in unison*). It's your sisters!

CLAUDINE. We thought you'd like to see our clothes for the
ball.

CLAUDETTE. Claudine is wearing her red velvet with French
trimmimg.

CLAUDINE. And Claudette is wearing her best silk that
Daddy brought from market.

CLAUDINE *and* CLAUDETTE (*in unison*). Aren't we lovely?

ISABELLA. No!

CLAUDINE *and* CLAUDETTE (*in unison*). Oh yes we are!

AUDIENCE. Oh no you're not!

CLAUDINE *and* CLAUDETTE (*in unison*). Oh yes we are!

AUDIENCE. Oh no you're not!

CLAUDINE and CLAUDETTE (*in unison*).
We don't care what you think
We're OK and you stink!

ISABELLA. That's my haircomb, and those are my bracelets!

CLAUDETTE. So? They look much better on us.

CLAUDINE. And anyway, you won't be needing them.

CLAUDETTE. Just think – We'll dance with The Prince, and you Isabella, you'll dance with . . .

CLAUDINE *and* CLAUDETTE (*in unison, pointing at* BOY). Him!

They laugh loudly, surround the BOY.

CLAUDINE. Look at the smelly, little kitchen boy.

CLAUDETTE (*poking the* BOY). You are smelly, aren't you?

CLAUDINE (*poking the* BOY). And you're dirty too, aren't you?

ISABELLA. Leave him alone!

CLAUDINE. He's so dirty you can't see his face.

CLAUDETTE (*straight to his face*). You must be really stupid to get so dirty.

CLAUDINE. He's so stupid he can't even speak!

ISABELLA. He can speak when he wants to! And he's only dirty because he does all the hardest work.

CLAUDETTE. And look at her! Look at proud Isabella now!

CLAUDINE. She's nearly as dirty as him!

CLAUDETTE. Messyella!

CLAUDINE. Stinkabella!

CLAUDETTE. Smellyella!

CLAUDINE (*emptying some ashes over her head*). Sootyella!

CLAUDETTE. Cinderella! That's it – we'll call her Cinderella!

CLAUDINE. She doesn't deserve a proper name any more because she's not a proper person any more!

CINDERELLA *turns away, hurt.*

CLAUDETTE (*delighted*). Look – she's going to cry.

CLAUDINE (*delighted*). The little baby.

BOY. Don't talk to her like that!

CLAUDETTE. He's found his tongue.

CLAUDINE. Well he'd better lose it again.

CLAUDINE *and* CLAUDETTE (*in unison*). Or else!

BOY. I'm not scared of you.

CLAUDINE. Come over here and say that.

BOY *moves towards her.*

CLAUDETTE. He's coming over, Claudine.

CLAUDINE. So he is, Claudette.

BOY (*straight to her face*). I said – I'm not scared of you!

Enter CLAUDIA, *in full sail, terrifying.*

CLAUDIA. WELL YOU SHOULD BE YOU HORRIBLE LITTLE BRAT! IF I EVER CATCH YOU TALKING TO HER LIKE THAT AGAIN I'LL HAVE YOU HUNG UP BY YOUR EARS! (*Softly.*) Come to mother, my little treasures. (CLAUDINE *and* CLAUDETTE *run to her embrace.*) Was he bad to you, my lambs?

CLAUDINE (*all pathetic*). He was.

CLAUDIA. And was Isabella bad to you too?

CLAUDETTE (*all pathetic*). She's always bad, except she's not called Isabella any more.

CLAUDINE. She's Cinderella now.

CLAUDIA. Oh yes, that's a much better name for her. What clever girls you are. (*Claps her hands loudly.*) Sergeant Puff, come here immediately! (PUFF *enters at a run, napkin at his neck, stands to attention.*) Now, Sergeant Puff, the girl has a new name. She is to be called Cinderella at all times. Is that understood?

PUFF (*totally respectful*). Yes, Your Importance.

CLAUDIA. Good. And have you done what I told you? Has she been worked hard, and made to sleep on the stone floor?

PUFF. She has, Your Bigness.

CLAUDIA. Very good. And I trust a feast has been prepared?

PUFF. Of course, Your Great Bigness.

CLAUDIA. Show me!

    PUFF *uncovers the trays of food.*

CLAUDINE. Oh mama, look – it's wonderful.

CLAUDETTE. I'll never be able to hang on.

CLAUDIA. It will do, Puff. Have it all taken upstairs.

PUFF. At once, Your Hugeness. (*He signals urgently off. The* WORKERS *enter, quickly, anxious to please.*) Hurry, men . . . Careful! At the double now . . . Watch out! That's the way, boys . . . mind what you're doing! (*The* WORKERS *get trays up on to their shoulders.*) By the left, quick march.

CLAUDETTE. Mama, mama! Can we have some now?

CLAUDINE. Can we, mama?

CLAUDIA. Of course you can . . . Help yourselves.

CLAUDINE (*rudely, to* WORKER). Stop!

    He stops.

CLAUDETTE. Down!

    He kneels, so they can survey the tray. They make their choice, after some brief agonising.

CLAUDINE. Up!

    He stands.

CLAUDETTE. Go!

He follows other WORKERS *off.*

CLAUDINE *and* CLAUDETTE *guzzle their food, groaning with pleasure.*

CINDERELLA (*to* BOY). I wish you had spat on them.

CLAUDINE. Yumptious!

CLAUDETTE. Scrumptious!

CLAUDIA. Look at all you're missing, Cinderella – and all because you can't be a good girl.

CINDERELLA. What difference would it make?

CLAUDIA *shares a look with* CLAUDETTE *and* CLAUDINE.

CLAUDIA. Oh well, if you were to be a really good girl, well, we might let you . . .

CINDERELLA. Go to the ball? Would you let me go?

CLAUDINE. We might.

CLAUDETTE. You never know.

CINDERELLA. But you would never let me go, that's silly . . . You wouldn't, would you? But if I was a good . . . If I was a really good girl, you might let me go, you said so. (*Steeling herself.*) Very well, I will be a good girl . . . And then will you promise to let me go?

CLAUDIA. Oh yes, I promise.

CINDERELLA (*eagerly*). Tell me how to be good, tell me.

CLAUDIA. Respect, Cinderella! You must respect your elders and betters! And you must be polite at all times. Is that understood?

CINDERELLA. Yes.

CLAUDIA. Yes, Lady Claudia.

CINDERELLA (*with difficulty*). Yes, Lady Claudia.

CLAUDIA. Good girl . . . See how easy it is.

CLAUDINE. And how do I look, Cinderella? Am I lovely?

CINDERELLA. You are lovely, Claudine.

CLAUDETTE. And what about me?

CINDERELLA. You are lovely too, Claudette.

CLAUDINE. Not more lovely, I hope!

CINDERELLA. Oh no – it is impossible to say who is lovelier.

CLAUDETTE. My dress is a little loose at the back.

CINDERELLA. I will see to it. (*Repairs it.*) There you are.

CLAUDINE. A curl has fallen over my ear.

CINDERELLA. I will pin it up. (*Pins it up.*) There.

CLAUDIA. There is dust on my shoe.

CINDERELLA. Then I will clean your shoe. (*Kneels and wipes dust away.*) It is clean again.

CLAUDIA. You can be quite a good girl when you try, can't you?

CINDERELLA. Yes.

CLAUDIA. Ah-ah?

CINDERELLA. Yes, Lady Claudia.

CLAUDIA. Better.

CINDERELLA. And since I'm good, will you . . . Will you let me go to the royal ball? (SERGEANT PUFF *wipes his forehead with his napkin, The* BOY *looks away – they know what's coming.*) Please.

CLAUDIA (*with her prettiest smile*). Oh no, I don't think so.

CLAUDINE. You can't dance!

CLAUDETTE. You've got no clothes!

CLAUDIA. Everyone would laugh at you! You'd make us ashamed.

CINDERELLA. But you promised!

CLAUDIA. Yes, but a promise to you doesn't count.

CLAUDETTE. She really thought we would let her go.

CLAUDINE. The stupid little baby.

CINDERELLA. HOW COULD I BE SO STUPID! TO
THINK THAT I LET MYSELF BELIEVE THEM!
I'LL NEVER LET THAT HAPPEN AGAIN IN THE
REST OF MY LIFE! NEVER, NEVER, NEVER AGAIN!
(*Enter* FATHER, *unseen by* CINDERELLA.) GET OUT OF
HERE – ALL OF YOU! YOU ONLY CAME HERE TO
LAUGH AT ME! I HATE YOU – I HATE YOU ALL!

FATHER (*sternly*). What's going on here?

> PUFF, *only now seeing* FATHER, *springs to attention.*

CLAUDINE. She's being horrible.

CLAUDETTE. We were only trying to be nice, and she bit our
heads off.

CINDERELLA (*furious, to herself*). They've done it again!

FATHER. It's a pity . . . I was hoping she could come to the
ball.

> CINDERELLA *turns away, won't look at him.*

CLAUDIA. That's quite impossible. The girl's worse than ever.
Come, my treasures – we must get ready to welcome The
Prince! (*Exits.*)

CLAUDINE (*to* CINDERELLA). We are sorry you can't
come.

CLAUDETTE (*to* CINDERELLA). We hope you get better
soon.

> *Exeunt* CLAUDINE *and* CLAUDETTE, *after curtseying
> dutifully and prettily to* FATHER.

FATHER. I'm very disappointed in you, you know that don't
you? (*She won't look at him.*) I've brought something for
you . . . Here . . . It's what you asked for – a branch from
your tree.

> *He holds the branch out to her, but she refuses to take it.*

PUFF. I'll see she gets it, sir. (*Takes branch.*)

FATHER. Thank you, Sergeant Puff . . . And how's the boy? (*To* BOY.) Are you behaving yourself?

The BOY *stares defiantly at* FATHER, *refuses to answer.*

PUFF. The Lord-General's speaking to you! (*Urgently.*) Speak up, boy – speak up! (*Still nothing.*) He's behaving very well, sir – most of the time.

FATHER. Very good. Goodnight, sergeant.

PUFF. Goodnight, sir. (*Exit* FATHER.) You'll be the finish of me – the pair of you!

CINDERELLA *sits down by the hearth, utterly miserable.*

BOY. I won't call you Cinderella.

PUFF. You'll do what you're told! Here, girl.

He gives branch to CINDERELLA. *She takes it and cherishes it.*

BOY. I don't care what we're told . . . I'll use her real name.

CINDERELLA. No, I'm Cinderella now! Everything I do is wrong . . . I'm Cinderella . . .

PUFF (*sadly, shaking his head*). Life is no laughing-matter. (*Opens cupboard. To* BOY.) In you get – bedtime!

BOY. I'm coming . . . (*Kneels beside* CINDERELLA.) Remember, Cinderella – there are demons in the ovens and ghosts in the chimney.

CINDERELLA. Don't.

BOY. Hobgoblins in the corners, and spirits in the air.

PUFF. You'll give her nightmares.

BOY. But the darkest, the blackest of all night's creatures – that's The Black Douglas!

PUFF (*catching on*). It's true! Just hearing his name makes me shiver . . . The Black Douglas! (*Shivers.*)

PUFF *exits.*

BOY. The Black Douglas wanders the corridors of the castle, his teeth shining in the dark, his breath like fire. And sometimes he comes here to the kitchen to steal meat!

CINDERELLA. I'll die if someone isn't kind to me.

BOY. What's that? I'm sure I heard something . . . It's him!
I'm sure of it – he's coming!

CINDERELLA (*covering her eyes*). Don't let him find me.

BOY. The Black Douglas is coming!

Enter PUFF *looking back and off with terrified eyes. He is
followed by* THE BLACK DOUGLAS, *a large, shaggy,
black dog.*

PUFF (*kindly, to dog*). Away and say hullo, you big lump.

CINDERELLA *uncovers her eyes.* THE BLACK
DOUGLAS *bounds over to her, welcomes her, licks her
face.*

CINDERELLA (*laughing*). So you're The Black Douglas.
(*Dog barks.*) Good boy . . . Stop licking!

BOY. Good boy, Dougie . . . I found him stealing food from
the bins. He was so skinny he could hardly stand . . . Now
look at him.

CINDERELLA. He's huge, and he's lovely . . . Look at his
ears.

BOY (*holding dog's ears back*). It's The Lugless Douglas!

CINDERELLA (*to* THE BLACK DOUGLAS). Is he being
cruel to you? (*Dog barks.*) Yes, he is. (*Hugs dog.*)

PUFF (*to* BOY). You're far too soft! That dog gets the run of
the place!

BOY. I saw you this morning – you gave him half your
breakfast.

PUFF. Nonsense! The brute took it when I wasn't looking.

BOY. That's your story.

CINDERELLA. I'd give him my breakfast too . . . Paw. (*Gets
paw.*) Other paw. (*Gets other paw.*) You really are a very
good dog. (*Dog barks.*) I see you. (*To* AUDIENCE.) Will I
get him to say hullo to you?

AUDIENCE. Yes.

CINDERELLA. On you go then, Dougie . . . You bark at them, and they'll bark at you. (THE BLACK DOUGLAS *turns away. To* AUDIENCE.) He doesn't believe me. . . . You will bark back, won't you?

AUDIENCE. Yes.

CINDERELLA (*to* THE BLACK DOUGLAS). There you are. Go on now – say hullo.

THE BLACK DOUGLAS *barks.*

AUDIENCE. Woof.

CINDERELLA (*to* THE BLACK DOUGLAS). Again.

THE BLACK DOUGLAS *barks, twice.*

AUDIENCE. Woof, woof.

CINDERELLA. Clever dog.

PUFF (*yawning and stretching*). Well, I'm for my bed. (*To* THE BLACK DOUGLAS.) Come on, fleabag . . . Goodnight . . .

BOY. Sergeant Puff, can he stay here with me? Please, can he?

PUFF. Oh, I don't know – he's a secret, remember . . . They wouldn't like it upstairs if they knew there was a dog in the kitchen.

CINDERELLA. We wouldn't tell them.

PUFF. All right, then . . . On you go, Dougie. (*Dog runs to* BOY.)

BOY. Thanks, Sergeant Puff. (*Hugs dog.*) One day I'll make you laugh, I promise.

PUFF. If only you could . . . Now – bedtime! Everybody get to bed. There's work to be done – first thing in the morning! (*The* BOY *and* THE BLACK DOUGLAS *enter cupboard.* PUFF *shuts the door, picks up oil lamp.*) Goodnight, one and all! (*Exits with lamp.*)

CINDERELLA *kneels by the light of the fire, which makes shapes on the walls.*

CINDERELLA. I miss my room and my warm bed. I wish . . . but that's just stupid . . . I won't be scared tonight, I won't let myself be scared!

VOICE (*a whisper*). Cinderella.

CINDERELLA (*starting with fright*). Who . . . who's that?

VOICE. Over here.

The BOY *and* THE BLACK DOUGLAS *have their heads out of the cupboard.*

CINDERELLA (*relaxing*). Oh, it's you.

BOY. I never told you . . . My name – it's Callum.

CINDERELLA. Callum . . . Goodnight, Callum.

CALLUM. Goodnight.

THE BLACK DOUGLAS *barks.*

CINDERELLA. And goodnight to The Black Douglas.

THE BLACK DOUGLAS *barks.*

CALLUM. Sleep tight.

CALLUM *and* THE BLACK DOUGLAS *return to cupboard, closing the door. Laughter and music can be heard in the distance – the sounds of the royal ball.*

CINDERELLA. Listen to them all enjoying themselves at the ball! Why should I care, when they don't care about me? But I do care. (*Holds the branch against her cheek.*) I wish . . . (*Kneels by the hearth, closes her eyes.*)

Moon light
Moon bright
New moon
Seen tonight
I wish I may
I wish I might
Have the wish
I wish tonight

Opens her eyes.

Nothing! What's the point in wishing when wishes never come true?

She throws the branch on the fire. It burns and flares with a magical light. The light and smoke clear to reveal the gentle, strong figure of THE FAIRY GODMOTHER.

FAIRY GODMOTHER. Do not be afraid, Cinderella.

CINDERELLA. Who . . . who are you?

FAIRY GODMOTHER. Think of me only as your friend. You were left in my care, and I have come to help you.

CINDERELLA (*timidly*). I won't be afraid.

FAIRY GODMOTHER. That's my girl. Trust me, and tell me what is your greatest wish.

CINDERELLA. I think you are my greatest wish . . . but I have another.

FAIRY GODMOTHER. Tell me it.

CINDERELLA. Oh, what's the use – I am too little and stupid.

FAIRY GODMOTHER. That's enough of that! You're better than the whole lot of them put together! Now, tell me your wish.

CINDERELLA. I wish . . . I wish I could go to the ball.

FAIRY GODMOTHER. Then you shall go to the ball.

CINDERELLA. But how? I have no clothes . . . Everyone would laugh at me.

FAIRY GODMOTHER. Just as you did not forget, so shall you not be forgotten.

CINDERELLA. I don't understand. Will you use magic?

FAIRY GODMOTHER. We will use your magic.

CINDERELLA. My magic?

FAIRY GODMOTHER. Yes . . . There is a tree that grows nearby. It is a magic tree, made so by your courage and your love . . . You must stand under your tree, let its leaves touch your hair, and speak the words –

Shake your leaves my little tree
Drop gold and silver down on me.

Let me hear you.

CINDERELLA.
Shake your leaves my little tree
Drop gold and silver down on me.

FAIRY GODMOTHER. Good girl – and the tree will dress you in clothes as beautiful as you deserve . . . Now go – but you must return by the midnight hour. At the last stroke of midnight all magic is spent and darkness is all . . . Do not forget.

CINDERELLA. I won't forget. (*Turning away.*) Please don't let this be a dream.

FAIRY GODMOTHER. I am no dream . . . Trust me.

She vanishes into the darkness.

CINDERELLA. I've hoped so much . . . (*Turns back.*) She's gone.

VOICE. Trust me.

Door opens by magic, the sounds of the ball grow louder.

CINDERELLA. Trust me . . . I will go to the tree! And I will go to the ball!

She exits through the door, which begins to close behind her, revealing THE FAIRY GODMOTHER.

FAIRY GODMOTHER.
I hear them at their fancy royal ball
Let's see how magic makes fools of them all!

The door closes. THE FAIRY GODMOTHER *vanishes into the darkness, and the transformation begins as if it has been commanded to by her magic.*

Scene Four

The main-hall, now serving as an ante-room to the adjoining great-hall, where the royal ball is being held. Everything is very grand and adult. The chandeliers are lit, ornate hangings adorn the walls. A huge armchair is piled high with capes and furs.

Loud music, and the sound of laughter and dancing. The dancers come into the main hall. Among them CLAUDIA, *full of self-importance, dances with* KING JOHN *and* CLAUDINE *and* CLAUDETTE *dance with each other.*

The music ceases, the dancers applaud, and bow to each other.

KING (*mopping his brow*). I'm too old for all this! I've lost the feeling in my legs.

CLAUDIA. Not at all, Your Highness. It's a pleasure to dance with you.

KING. If I was a horse I'd have been put down years ago. (*Polite laughter.*) Stop that polite laughter! That's all a king ever hears – polite laughter! Now I'm getting a headache. Where's my son, The Prince? He should be dancing, not me!

CLAUDINE (*dreamily*). He was at the feast.

CLAUDETTE (*dreamily*). At the top of our table.

CLAUDINE (*dreamily*). I couldn't stop looking at him.

CLAUDIA *kicks her.*

CLAUDETTE (*dreamily*). He's gorgeous.

CLAUDIA *kicks her.*

CLAUDINE. But when the dancing was about to start . . .

CLAUDETTE. And everyone was waiting to see who he would choose as his partner . . .

CLAUDINE. He ran away, and we can't find him anywhere!

KING. Typical! What that boy needs is a good kick up the . . . (*He is drowned out by a loud "Ah" of excited voices from the great-hall. CLAUDINE and CLAUDETTE rush to see what all the fuss is about.*)

CLAUDIA. Is it him? Is it The Prince?

CLAUDINE. Oh mama – it's a dancing-bear!

CLAUDETTE. He's beautiful! Come and see, come and see!

CLAUDIA. My treasures.

Exeunt all, save KING and CLAUDIA. Music begins in the great hall.

KING. Dancing-bears . . . I'm up to here with dancing-bears!

CLAUDIA. One little thing, Your Majesty . . . My daughters can think of nothing but dancing with Prince Rufus, the lambs . . . They get so excited . . . I hate to ask but do you think you could possibly . . . ?

KING. Leave it to me. I'll see that The Prince dances!

CLAUDIA. Thank you, Your Highness. (*She curtsies.*) And may I just say what an honour it is to have you in our castle.

Exit CLAUDIA.

KING. That woman makes my teeth hurt! But I'll make sure he dances! It's his duty! Oh yes, my boy, you'll dance tonight!

VOICE. Oh no I won't.

KING. Oh yes you will.

VOICE. Oh no I won't.

KING. Oh yes you . . . !!!

PRINCE RUFUS *emerges from under the furs and capes. He is eating an orange.*

PRINCE. I won't dance.

KING (*finally seeing him*). So there you are!

PRINCE. The Prince will not dance.

KING. The Prince will do what he's told!

PRINCE. Oh yes he will!

KING. Oh no he won't!

PRINCE. All right, father – you win.

KING (*making strangling motions*). Oh!!! But you have to dance. It's a royal ball and you're The Prince!

PRINCE. And you're The King . . . Ban dancing . . . No more dancing, by royal decree.

KING. Don't get clever with me! People have come from all over – the most beautiful girls in the country. The least you can do is dance!

PRINCE. I won't dance, father! I won't dance because there is no-one I want to dance with.

KING. Come here! (*Grabs* THE PRINCE.)

PRINCE. Let go!

KING. Over here! (*Faces* PRINCE towards ballroom, points out dancers in the great hall) There's the young Lady Windermere . . . What's wrong with her?

PRINCE. Too tall.

KING. The Lady Glockenspiel?

PRINCE. Too small.

KING. That girl there – in the green?

PRINCE. I'd rather dance with the bear.

KING. That girl then – in the red.

PRINCE. I don't like her nose.

KING. She's got a lovely nose!

PRINCE. Then you dance with her.

KING (*cuffs* PRINCE). The Lady Claudia's daughters, Claudine and Claudette – they're beautiful.

PRINCE. Yes, but they think too much of themselves, and that spoils their beauty.

KING. Nothing makes you happy! You're the one who's spoiled, do you know that!

PRINCE. If I'm spoiled someone must have spoiled me . . . You should shout at yourself for doing the spoiling . . . I won't dance!

KING. Oh yes you will!

PRINCE. Oh no I won't!

KING (*hopping with fury*). I'm not going to have another one of these stupid arguments!

PRINCE. Oh yes you are.

KING. Oh no I'm not!

PRINCE. Oh yes you are.

KING. Oh no I'm . . . !!! Get into that ballroom! Go on! Get in there or else I'll pick you up and carry you!

PRINCE. I'll go, father . . . But a ballroom is the loneliest place in the world when there is no-one you want to dance with.

Exits to ballroom. Excited voices greet him, and the music too seems to swell with excitement.

KING. One day I'll explode and there'll be nothing left of me but a little golden crown rolling across the marble! (*Takes off his crown, blows on it, polishes it.*) Ah well, perhaps he's right . . . Perhaps there's no-one here to make a Prince dream, no-one to make a Prince dance.

Enter CINDERELLA, *looking over her shoulder, trying not to be seen. She collides with* KING.

KING. Watch where you're going!

CINDERELLA. Please excuse me.

KING. Consider yourself excused . . . Are you all right?

CINDERELLA. Yes, thank you.

KING. It could have been worse.

CINDERELLA. I know – I could have bumped into The King. (KING *puts crown on.*) You are The King! I'm sorry, I've never met a King before . . . I don't know what to say.

KING. Let's see . . . How about – Hullo, King. Try that.

CINDERELLA (*awkwardly*). Hullo, King.

KING. That'll do splendidly . . . Pleased to meet you. (*Shakes her hand.*) What's your name?

CINDERELLA. My name? Oh well . . . my name! Well, it's . . .

KING. You must be a Princess.

CINDERELLA. A Princess? Oh no . . .

KING. Only a Princess could wear such fine clothes. Where do you come from?

CINDERELLA. Come from? Well, you see . . .

KING. I've never seen you before. You must come from somewhere very far away.

CINDERELLA. No . . . Yes . . . if you say so.

KING. But how could I have missed you? Were you at the ball?

CINDERELLA. I've been there for hours . . . Everyone was dancing when I arrived, so I hid over by the window.

KING. And you didn't dance?

CINDERELLA. Oh no, but I watched everyone else, and I listened to them talking and laughing, and I saw the bear dancing . . . It's been wonderful, I've seen everything . . . Except for The Prince.

KING. You haven't missed much.

CINDERELLA. He's all they talk about.

KING. Then come with me and I'll introduce you to The Prince. (*Takes her hand.*)

CINDERELLA. Oh no, I couldn't . . .

KING. He won't bite.

CINDERELLA (*pulling away*). Really, I couldn't.

A commotion from the ballroom, voices raised in argument.

KING. You'll see him now, for here he comes.

CINDERELLA. It's late . . . I must go.

She tries to go but the KING *holds her back.*

KING. Hide, then – if you're shy . . . Over there, go on. You're good at hiding. (*He pushes her into hiding.*) I'll look after you.

Enter CLAUDIA, CLAUDINE *and* CLAUDETTE *who have hold of* THE PRINCE.

CLAUDIA (*to daughters, obsessively*). Don't let him go! He's yours and no-one else's! (*Sees* KING, *tries to lighten it.*) The treasures.

CLAUDINE (*to* PRINCE). You'll dance with me, won't you?

CLAUDETTE (*to* PRINCE). And then you'll dance with me. (*Almost twisting his arm.*) I know you will!

PRINCE. I won't dance! Help, father!

CLAUDIA. No-one must dance with him except my daughters!

CLAUDINE *and* CLAUDETTE (*in unison*). We're lovely!

Some unseemly wrestling.

PRINCE. Help me, father! Help me!

KING. My lords, ladies and gentlemen, I give you – (*Pulls* CINDERELLA *out of hiding.*) – The Princess Faraway.

A great silence falls. All admire CINDERELLA, *and perhaps we hear* – *'How handsome she is,' 'How beautiful.'* THE PRINCE *steps forward.*

PRINCE. How pleased I am to see you. Welcome, Princess Faraway. (*He bows to her.*)

CINDERELLA (*awkwardly*). Hullo, Prince.

All laugh.

CLAUDINE. What a silly way to address His Royal Majesty.

PRINCE. From now on it shall be the only way!

KING (*laughing*). Well spoken.

All press forward, gazing at her, touching her.

CLAUDINE. Feel her clothes.

CLAUDETTE. And her hair.

CLAUDINE. And look at her shoes – they're made of glass.

CLAUDETTE. I've never seen anything so beautiful.

CLAUDIA (*fingering her dress, with a stern gaze*). You must tell us where to find the cloth, so we may have some made after the fashion.

CINDERELLA (*meeting her gaze*). You're very kind, but even if you found the cloth you could never find the hands to stitch it.

PRINCE. Come . . . I will talk to you – alone! (*He pulls her away from the crowd, into a magical light that separates them from the others, who all strain to hear, reporting what they can in eager whispers.*) I have been to a hundred balls, and I never thought I would find you . . . Oh Princess Faraway, I wish . . . I wish . . .

CINDERELLA. What do you wish?

PRINCE. I wish I had met you sooner, and we could have danced every dance together, for I would have no other partner . . . Let me give you these instead.

He takes a pouch from his belt.

CINDERELLA. What are they?

PRINCE. Oranges and lemons – my ships have brought them all the way from Spain.

CINDERELLA. They are rarer than gold.

PRINCE. Take them – it is my gift to you.

CINDERELLA. I have nothing to give in return.

PRINCE. Give me your hand . . . (*She hesitates.*) You are afraid . . . You are afraid that if I kiss your hand, I will kiss your arm, and if I kiss your arm, then I may kiss your shoulder, and then . . .

CINDERELLA. I am not afraid.

She gives him her hand, and he kisses it gently, and then lets go of it. The magical light fades.

CLAUDETTE. A present, a present!

CLAUDINE. What is it?

CLAUDIA. Tell us, tell us!

CINDERELLA. Oranges and lemons.

CLAUDINE. I love oranges!

CLAUDETTE. So do I!

CLAUDINE. But really it is our sister who loves them best.

CLAUDETTE. Is it? (CLAUDINE *kicks her.*) Oh yes, of course it is.

CLAUDINE. Our poor little sister is too ill to come to the ball.

CLAUDETTE. The poor thing, but how a gift of oranges would cheer her up.

CINDERELLA. Then I will keep one – (*She takes an orange.*) – and you must give the rest to your poor sister.

PRINCE. You are as kind as you are beautiful.

CLAUDINE (*snatching pouch greedily*). Give them to me!

CINDERELLA. Not so kind as you imagine.

KING. Ladies and gentlemen – it is time for The Last Waltz.

PRINCE. The Last Waltz – then The Prince will dance! I will tell the musicians what to play. (*Exits, at a run.*)

CLAUDINE *and* CLAUDETTE (*in unison*). He's going to dance, he's going to dance! (*Suddenly terrified.*) But who with?

CINDERELLA. What's going on?

KING. He will tell the musicians to play The Midnight Waltz, and he will dance it with you, Princess. (*He bows to her.*) It is a great honour. (*Exits.*)

CLAUDINE *and* CLAUDETTE *commence banging their heads against a wall.* CLAUDIA *prays.*

CINDERELLA. That will be lovely . . . The Midnight Waltz! (*Clock begins to strike twelve.*) I'm sorry, Prince, but I have to go before the magic runs out! I have to go!

She exits, at a run.

CLAUDINE. She's gone!

CLAUDETTE. I don't believe it!

CLAUDIA. Sometimes I think we're looked after.

Enter PRINCE RUFUS. *The music begins.*

PRINCE. Listen to the music. I've never wanted to dance so much in all my life . . .

CLAUDINE *and* CLAUDETTE (*in unison*). Neither have we!

PRINCE. Princess? (*They grab his arms, drag him into the ballroom.*) Princess Faraway, where are you? Princess Farawaaaay . . .

CLAUDIA. My treasures. My little lambs.

She exits, after her treasures.

Scene Five

The castle kitchen. Dark and brooding, except for the warming light from the old hearth. The Midnight Waltz can be heard playing in the distance.

Enter CINDERELLA, *in her ragged dress.*

CINDERELLA. Cinderella again . . . It's so cold and dull when the magic runs out. (*Goes to hearth.*) But you're still burning, and I can still hear the music . . . They're dancing The Midnight Waltz. (*Dances a few steps.*) I'll never sleep. I'm too excited to sleep. (*Goes to cupboard, knocks on door.*) Wake up. (*Knocks again.*) Wake up . . .

CALLUM *comes out, in a wild rush.*

CALLUM. Am I late? I've got to clean the ovens, chop the wood. Hurry, hurry . . .

CINDERELLA. It's not morning yet . . . I only wanted to tell someone . . . I went to the ball . . . I did, I went to the royal ball!

CALLUM (*irritated, sleepy*). I don't believe it!

CINDERELLA. A woman came to me . . . She was kind, and told me to go to my mother's tree . . . The tree heard the magic words and it dressed me in clothes so beautiful they all thought I was a princess.

CALLUM. Go back to sleep!

CINDERELLA. It really happened! (*Relishing the memory.*) No-one knew it was me . . . I met The King, and then The Prince . . . He bowed to me, and he kissed my hand . . . Listen to the music. Come on – dance. (*Pulls* CALLUM *to his feet.*) Dance with me.

CALLUM. I can't dance.

CINDERELLA. I'll show you. 1-2-3 and . . .

They dance The Midnight Waltz, briefly and a little clumsily.

CALLUM (*pulling away*). I told you – I can't dance!

THE BLACK DOUGLAS *comes sleepily out of the cupboard, stretches luxuriously.*

CINDERELLA. Did I wake The Black Douglas too? I'm sorry. Come here, and I'll pat you. (*But he walks right past her to the hearth.*) What's the matter? (*The music stops.*)

CALLUM. He hates being woken up. (THE BLACK DOUGLAS *keels over by the hearth in a dead sleep.*) Quite right, Dougie. (*He lies down, his head on* THE BLACK DOUGLAS.)

CINDERELLA. The music's stopped anyway . . . The ball's over. (*Pause, then excited again.*) And The King gave me a name – Princess Faraway!

CALLUM. Stop it, Cinderella! It was all just a dream!

CINDERELLA. It wasn't a dream! Look. (*She takes out the orange.*) I brought you this.

CALLUM (*taking the orange*). What is it?

CINDERELLA. I've only had one once before. It's an orange. Taste it – they're delicious. (CALLUM *bites into it, spits with disgust.*) Not like that. (*Takes it back.*) Like this. (*Cuts it in half with a kitchen knife.*) Half for you, half for me . . . Now taste it.

She eats, he copies her.

CALLUM. It is delicious. (*Eats hungrily.*)

CINDERELLA. Thank you, Cinderella . . . Thank you for remembering me.

CALLUM. Thank you, Cinderella.

CINDERELLA. You gave me your bread. (*They eat.*) Now do you believe me?

CALLUM. I might.

A horrid babbling from off.

CINDERELLA. It's my sisters!

CALLUM. Quickly – hide The Black Douglas!

CINDERELLA. Come on, you big lump – get up! He won't move – he's too comfy.

CALLUM. Cover him, then. Hurry!

They cover THE BLACK DOUGLAS *with old flour sacks. He looks up, puzzled.* CALLUM *pushes his head down, covers it. Enter* CLAUDINE *and* CLAUDETTE.

CLAUDINE *and* CLAUDETTE (*in unison*). Guess who?

CLAUDINE. We thought you'd like to hear about the royal ball.

CLAUDETTE. You must be dying to know.

CINDERELLA. Oh yes, I am. Please tell me . . .

CLAUDINE. It was beautiful!

CLAUDETTE. Only the best people were invited!

CLAUDINE. And The Prince sat at our table!

CLAUDETTE. He's absolutely gorgeous!

CLAUDINE. And that's not all – we met a princess!

CLAUDETTE. We really did – The Princess Faraway!

THE BLACK DOUGLAS *lifts his head under the sack, and we can sense his puzzlement.*

CALLUM. Princess Faraway?

CLAUDINE. Who asked you?

CLAUDETTE. Keep your runny nose out of it!

CINDERELLA (*pushing* THE BLACK DOUGLAS *down with her foot*). And what was she like, this Princess Faraway?

CLAUDETTE. Oh you should have seen her.

CLAUDINE. She was beautiful.

CINDERELLA. Very beautiful?

CLAUDINE. Nearly as beautiful as us!

CLAUDETTE. And that's saying something!

CLAUDINE. But the best's still to come.

CLAUDETTE. Wait till you hear this.

CLAUDINE *and* CLAUDETTE (*in unison*). The Prince – he danced with us!

THE BLACK DOUGLAS *lifts his head.*

CLAUDINE. You never missed yourself so much in all your life!

CINDERELLA. I know . . . How lucky you are.

CALLUM *pushes* THE BLACK DOUGLAS *back down with his foot.*

CLAUDETTE (*rounding on* CALLUM). And did clarty-lugs dance with Cinderella while we were dancing with The Prince?

CLAUDINE. Look – he's embarrassed . . . They did dance.

CLAUDETTE. Don't they look good together?

CLAUDINE. One's as stupid and ugly as the other!

CLAUDETTE. And The Prince has asked mama to give another ball.

CINDERELLA. Another ball?

CLAUDINE. Isn't it wonderful? Some say it's because The Prince hopes Princess Faraway will come.

CLAUDETTE. But we know it's really because he wants to see us again.

CLAUDINE. What a perfect night!

CLAUDETTE. All that fun – and a sack of oranges to guzzle!

Shows the sack teasingly to CINDERELLA.

CLAUDINE. The Prince gave them to us.

CINDERELLA. He gave them to you?

CLAUDETTE. Why shouldn't he?

CLAUDINE. Since he liked us the best.

CINDERELLA. Won't you give me even one orange?

CLAUDETTE. Say please.

CINDERELLA. Please.

CLAUDINE. No!

CLAUDINE *and* CLAUDETTE (*in unison*). We're giving them to us!

CLAUDINE. Goodnight!

CLAUDETTE. And good riddance!

They leave, laughing, making a great show of their prize of oranges and lemons.

CINDERELLA. Now I know what liars they really are!

CALLUM. Why didn't you tell them you were at the ball?

CINDERELLA. It's my secret. They would only try to take it away from me.

CALLUM. Now I'm wide awake.

CINDERELLA (*yawning*). And I'm so sleepy . . . (*Lifts sack from* THE BLACK DOUGLAS.) You'll have to move, Dougie – that's where I sleep.

CALLUM. Come on, Dougie – move yourself.

THE BLACK DOUGLAS *gets sleepily to his feet, stands in a daze.* CINDERELLA *lies down by the hearth.*

CINDERELLA. You're a good dog.

THE BLACK DOUGLAS *keels over with a thump – out cold.*

CALLUM. Come on, Douglas!

CINDERELLA. Let him stay with me . . . Just this once.

CALLUM. Just this once . . . I'll get you a blanket.

CALLUM *goes into his cupboard.* CINDERELLA *places her head on* THE BLACK DOUGLAS.

CINDERELLA. So sleepy . . . I can't keep my eyes open . . .

THE FAIRY GODMOTHER *appears by the hearth.*

FAIRY GODMOTHER. I came to wish you goodnight.

CINDERELLA (*sleepily*). You're here . . . I'm glad you're here. But Callum – he'll see you . . .

FAIRY GODMOTHER. I am invisible to him. (*Enter* CALLUM *with blanket. He walks right past* THE FAIRY GODMOTHER.) He can neither see nor hear me.

CALLUM *covers* CINDERELLA *with the blanket.*

CALLUM. Work starts well before it's light.

FAIRY GODMOTHER. You are kind, for one who has so little.

CINDERELLA. So he is.

CALLUM. What are you saying now?

CINDERELLA. Nothing . . . You're kind . . . Thank you.

THE FAIRY GODMOTHER *blows on* CALLUM's *neck.*

CALLUM (*shivers*). Spirits in the air!

CINDERELLA. Goodnight, Callum.

CALLUM. Goodnight, princess . . . Sleep tight.

He enters the cupboard, closes the door.

CINDERELLA (*almost asleep*). The clothes were lovely . . . Thank you . . . I never thought I could go . . . Everyone . . . Even my father . . . They thought I was a princess . . . And The Prince . . . The Prince has asked for another ball . . .

FAIRY GODMOTHER. And you shall go to it.

CINDERELLA. He kissed my hand . . .

FAIRY GODMOTHER.
Moon light
Moon bright
New moon
Seen tonight
I wish you may
I wish you might
Have the wish
You wish tonight

CINDERELLA. He kissed my hand . . . he gave me oranges.

FAIRY GODMOTHER. Shhhh . . . Go to sleep, Cinderella. (*Kisses her.*) Go to sleep.

CINDERELLA *sleeps.* THE FAIRY GODMOTHER *withdraws slowly, vanishes into the darkness.*

Curtain.

ACT TWO

Scene One

The castle kitchen. The WORKERS *prepare food for the royal
ball.* THE BLACK DOUGLAS *sits contentedly by the hearth.*
SERGEANT PUFF *moves among his* WORKERS.

PUFF. Hurry, hurry!
    Stir the soup, scrub the floor
    That goes there, behind the door
    Hurry, hurry!
    Move yourself, don't tell me you're tired
    Salt in that water, more wood on the fire.

He warms himself by the hearth, scratches THE BLACK
DOUGLAS' *ears.* CALLUM *and* CINDERELLA *enter with
sacks of flour.* CINDERELLA *manages hers with ease,
stowing it in a corner.*

That's the way! Good girl! (CALLUM *watches him
scratching the dog's ears.* PUFF *stops, embarrassed.*) Daft
lump!

Hurry, hurry!
Heads down, don't let that fall
We've got to make the food for the royal ball
Hurry, hurry!
Whatever you do, for all of your sakes
Don't let me forget about my lovely cake.

ALL. Your cake!

PUFF. Oh no! I've forgotten about my cake! Out of the way!
(*Rushes to oven, takes out cake tin.*) Ah, my beauty – you're
perfect. (*All sigh with relief.*) When all the great people at
the ball see you they will say how Sergeant Puff bakes the
best cakes in the whole wide world.

He exits with cake. Immediately the WORKERS *form a
huddle.*

CINDERELLA. What are they doing?

CALLUM. Planning their trick. One day every month we try to make the Sergeant laugh . . . Today's that day. What's your trick?

CINDERELLA. I don't have one.

CALLUM. Neither do I . . . We've got to think of something.

CINDERELLA. I can't think about anything except the ball.

CALLUM. Who cares about the ball?

CINDERELLA. I care! I'm sure I can go again – if I trust in the magic.

CALLUM (*scornfully*). The magic! I hate them all up there.

CINDERELLA. You're just jealous because you can't go.

CALLUM. I'd rather make the sergeant laugh.

CINDERELLA. Oh, but The Prince . . . He kissed my hand . . .

CALLUM. I know, I know – and he gave you oranges. He's all you ever talk about.

CINDERELLA. Why shouldn't I? He's tall and handsome . . .

CALLUM (*anticipating her*). And he has such lonely eyes.

CINDERELLA. And he has such lonely eyes . . . !!!

CALLUM. Surprise, surprise, he's got lonely eyes!

CINDERELLA. You're horrible!

CALLUM. So are you!

CINDERELLA. Kitchen boy!

CALLUM. Princess!

Enter SERGEANT PUFF. *The* WORKERS *present themselves with confidence, and prepare to perform their trick.*

PUFF. Oh no, it's not that time again, is it? Come on then, let's get it over with . . . Come on, or we'll be here all day!

The WORKERS *perform their trick.* WORKER *1 fills bellows with water from a bucket.* WORKER 2 *assumes the exaggerated posture of a 'fountain angel'.* WORKER 1 *holds the bellows against* WORKER 2's *backside, and squeezes the bellows. A jet of water shoots out of* WORKER 2's *mouth, and is caught in a bucket by* WORKER 3, *who bows to* PUFF. CALLUM *and* CINDERELLA *laugh, but* PUFF *remains unmoved.*

Is that it? You mean, you've finished? (WORKERS *sag with disappointment.*) Right – back to work!

CALLUM. I've got a trick, Sergeant Puff.

CINDERELLA (*eagerly*). What is it, what is it?

CALLUM. This!

He slaps a pie hard into CINDERELLA's *face. She is speechless. The* WORKERS *laugh,* PUFF *does not.*

PUFF. So you think that's funny, do you? Well, I don't. (*Smashes egg on* WORKER's *head.*) And I don't think that's funny! (*Pushes next* WORKER *over dog, empties bucket over his head.*) And that's not funny either! (*Empties saucepan down trousers of next* WORKER.) That's not funny! (*Puts pan over* WORKER's *head and bangs it with a spoon.*) And that's definitely not funny!

CALLUM (*laughing*). Well, I think it's funny.

CINDERELLA. Oh, do you?

She slaps a pie hard into CALLUM's *face. He is speechless. The* WORKERS *laugh.*

PUFF (*the merest flicker of a laugh*). Now that . . . That nearly . . . No, it's gone! What's the use? It's good of you all to try but when I don't laugh it only reminds me THAT LIFE IS NO LAUGHING-MATTER! SO GET ON WITH YOUR WORK! I'VE GOT TO MAKE THE ICING! THE CAKE MUST BE PERFECT! HURRY, HURRY!

PUFF *and the* WORKERS *return to work.*

CINDERELLA. I'm sorry, Callum. (*They wipe each other's faces.*)

CALLUM. You nearly made him laugh, and anyway – I was asking for it.

CINDERELLA. So was I. (*They shake hands.* THE BLACK DOUGLAS *barks.*)

CALLUM. What is it, Dougie?

CINDERELLA. Someone's coming . . . It's my father!

PUFF. The Lord-General! Everybody, look your best! Atteeeen-tion! (*They stand to attention.* THE BLACK DOUGLAS *stretches lazily, in clear view.*) The dog! Hide the dog! (CALLUM *covers* THE BLACK DOUGLAS *with an old sack. Enter* FATHER.) Good evening, sir!

FATHER. Good evening, sergeant. Everything in good order, I see.

PUFF. Couldn't be better, sir!

FATHER. Good . . . Very good. (*Sits on* THE BLACK DOUGLAS.) I've been sent to remind you about the cake.

PUFF. The cake, sir? Oh yes, sir. Baked as ordered, sir.

FATHER. Well done, and The Lady Claudia would like you to present it in person.

PUFF. Oh not me, sir. Not in front of all those grand people.

FATHER. That's an order, Sergeant Puff!

PUFF. Yes, sir!

FATHER (*stands*). You've worked hard – all of you. (*Indicates* CINDERELLA.) Not that she'll have been much help, I'm sure of that.

PUFF. She works hard all day long, sir, and never has to be told a thing twice. She's one of the best workers I've ever had.

FATHER. You can't be talking about my daughter?

PUFF. Yes, sir – your daughter.

FATHER. I don't believe it! I'll have to sit down. (*He goes to sit.* THE BLACK DOUGLAS *moves. He falls to the floor.*) What's going on? That's not a seat. (*Pulls sack off.*) That's a dog! (THE BLACK DOUGLAS *licks his face.*) He's licking my face! Get him off!

CALLUM *and* CINDERELLA *pull* THE BLACK DOUGLAS *away.*

PUFF (*to* WORKERS). Stop laughing at the General! (*To* FATHER.) Let me help you up, sir. (*To* WORKERS, *dropping* FATHER.) GET THAT FOOD TAKEN UPSTAIRS! MOVE YOURSELVES! (*They hurry to comply,* PUFF *helps* FATHER *up, brushes him down.*) What a thing to happen in my kitchen.

WORKERS *leave with trays of food.*

FATHER. Don't fuss, sergeant!

CINDERELLA. Don't blame The Black Douglas, father.

PUFF. It was our fault, sir – not the dog's.

CINDERELLA. Please don't take him away.

FATHER. Why should I do that? Anyone can see he's a harmless, big lump. Aren't you, eh? (*Pats him.*) The Black Douglas. Good boy . . . But don't let anyone else see him. Keep him hidden.

PUFF (*pleased*). Yes, sir. (*To* THE BLACK DOUGLAS.) On you go, flea-bag. (*Exit* THE BLACK DOUGLAS.)

CINDERELLA. Thank you, father.

FATHER. You're welcome . . . But there's still no royal ball for you! You'll need many more good reports from the sergeant before you're ready for that.

CINDERELLA. It's all right, father . . . I'll manage by myself.

FATHER (*to* CALLUM). And how's the wild boy? Are you happy in your work?

CALLUM *looks away, will not look at him.*

PUFF (*furious*). Stand up straight! Show some respect!

CALLUM. Never!

PUFF. I'll deal with him, sir. Come here . . .

FATHER. Leave him, sergeant . . . He may be my prisoner, but his thoughts are free.

PUFF. Sir.

FATHER. But remember – not everyone likes dogs.

PUFF. Yes, sir . . . Thank you, sir!

Exit FATHER.

(*To* CALLUM.) I'm warning you!

CINDERELLA. Why do you hate my father? Why are you a prisoner here?

CALLUM. Leave me alone.

PUFF (*mixing icing in a huge bowl*). Your father took him prisoner at the battle of the mountains. His mother is Warrior-Queen of all the northern tribes. As long as he is prisoner here, your father has power over the Queen, and there is no more war. That is why he can never go free.

CALLUM. I'll escape from here. One day I will!

PUFF. In your dreams! The castle walls are a hundred feet high.

CINDERELLA (*gently*). One day you will.

PUFF (*in a sudden panic*). But the ball – I've been ordered to go to the ball! I'll need my best uniform! And the cake! I've no time to make the icing!

CINDERELLA. We'll mix the icing, Sergeant Puff. On you go and get ready.

She takes the huge mixing-bowl and places it on the floor. She sits beside it and starts work.

PUFF. Thank you, Cinderella. A good stir now – no lumps! Just think – me, in front of all those grand people. My head's going round, I'm sick with nerves! (*Exits.*)

CINDERELLA. Come and help, Callum. (*She continues to stir.*) Please. (CALLUM *joins her, putting all his anger into the stirring.*) Careful! Not like that, or you'll spill it all. (*He slows down.*) That's it . . . That's better. (*They stir in unison.*) What's it like, far beyond the northern mountains?

CALLUM (*dourly*). It does nothing but rain.

CINDERELLA (*laughing*). It can't rain all the time. What are the people like?

CALLUM. Wet and cold.

CINDERELLA. I'm serious.

CALLUM. The people? Well, some of the time they think too much of themselves, but most of the time they think too little . . . But when the sun shines it shines down on the truest and bravest hearts in all the world.

CINDERELLA. You must miss them very much.

CALLUM. Keep stirring!

CINDERELLA. Not so fast. You're getting angry again.

CALLUM. I can't help it! I'd like to gather up all the dead spiders and rats from under the ovens! I'd crush them and mix them in so's you would never notice! Then I'd like to watch all the grand people eat the cake, piece by piece!

CINDERELLA. That's disgusting!

CALLUM. Or I'd spit in it – I told you I would. Or I could tickle my throat and be sick in beside it! That would be the best, except for the lumps.

CINDERELLA. You wouldn't really do that?

CALLUM. I would so! Come on, we could do it now! I'll get the spiders.

CINDERELLA. No you will not!

CALLUM. You're just scared.

CINDERELLA. I am not scared! I'm just not revolting like you.

CALLUM. Come on . . .

CINDERELLA. Nothing else is going in this bowl, and that's final! (THE BLACK DOUGLAS *enters, shambles over to the bowl, sniffs it.*) Douglas, what are you doing? Douglas . . . ? (THE BLACK DOUGLAS *'lifts his leg' over the side of the bowl.*) Look what he's doing!

CALLUM (*laughing*). He's not scared.

CINDERELLA (*scolding* THE BLACK DOUGLAS). You're a
dirty, dirty beast, so you are! Lie down! Go on – lie down!
What are we going to do?

CALLUM. Stir it in.

CINDERELLA. We can't do that.

CALLUM. Yes we can. (*He looks at her, until she nods her
agreement. They sit down by the bowl.*) Quickly – stir it in!
(*They stir in unison.*) No-one will know. (*Laughs with joy.*)

CINDERELLA. It's not funny.

CALLUM (*imitating* PUFF). Life is no laughing-matter!

They both laugh and continue to stir.

Enter SERGEANT PUFF, *in a rush. He is partially dressed
in his best uniform.*

PUFF. Hurry, hurry! Have you not finished yet?

CINDERELLA. It's finished, Sergeant Puff.

PUFF. Good for you. What are you laughing at?

CALLUM. Your uniform.

PUFF. What's wrong with my uniform?

CINDERELLA. You've forgotten your trousers.

PUFF. Don't be ridiculous! Of course I haven't . . . (*Looks
down.*) Oh no, I've forgotten my trousers! Help! I'll never
be ready in time!

CINDERELLA. Try not to hurry so much. Go and find your
trousers.

CALLUM. Then ice your cake. (*Hands him bowl.*) Here.

PUFF. Find my trousers, ice my cake! Right . . . Here, I hope
there's no lumps in this! I'd better taste it. (*Goes to taste it.*)

CINDERELLA. No! (*Stops him.*) You mustn't waste any.
Come on, and I'll find your trousers. (*She takes his hand.*)

PUFF. Outside my kitchen I'm like a drowning man . . .

CINDERELLA. You'll be fine. Come on.

They exit.

CALLUM *laughs, plays with* THE BLACK DOUGLAS.

CALLUM. You're the best dog in the world, Dougie . . . And she's . . . She's . . . Look, I've carved her a ring. (*Produces a ring from his pocket.*) What do you think? I hope she likes it . . . It's only made of wood – there's no gold or silver down here. I know it's daft, Dougie, but I can't give it to her . . . I don't know what to say . . .

Enter CINDERELLA.

CINDERELLA. I found his trousers, and he's icing the cake. Imagine if someone eats it! Yuk!

CALLUM (*awkwardly*). Cinderella?

CINDERELLA. What is it?

CALLUM. Well, you see . . . I thought . . . I'd like to . . . It's nothing . . . stupid! I wanted to . . .

The music from the ball starts, and can be heard in the distance.

CINDERELLA. Listen! They've started the dancing. It's lovely . . . (*Dances a few steps.*) What did you say?

CALLUM (*puts ring away*). Nothing.

CINDERELLA. I wonder what the magic will give me to wear. I hope I am more beautiful than my sisters.

CALLUM. Goodnight, Cinderella.

Exits to cupboard.

CINDERELLA. Oh please let me be more beautiful than them . . . Goodnight, Callum . . . But what if the magic has gone away and left me. (*Goes to hearth.*) Don't leave me. (*Closes eyes.*) Please be with me, magic . . . Please be with me . . .

THE FAIRY GODMOTHER *appears by magic.*

FAIRY GODMOTHER. I am with you always.

CINDERELLA. You make me strong.

FAIRY GODMOTHER. But listen to the music. You should be at the ball.

CINDERELLA. I was afraid the magic had gone away.

FAIRY GODMOTHER. How could it leave you when it is your own? You haven't forgotten the words you must tell the tree?

CINDERELLA. How could I forget?

Shake your leaves my little tree
Drop gold and silver down on me.

FAIRY GODMOTHER. Then you must go to the ball – (*She gestures, the door opens by magic.*) – if it is your wish.

CINDERELLA. Of course it is my wish. (*Runs towards door, stops.*) How could I wish for anything else? It's just that . . . There's something here . . . But that's silly . . . I will go! I must go!

FAIRY GODMOTHER. Don't forget – you must leave by the midnight hour.

CINDERELLA. I won't forget. (*She exits, at a run.*)

FAIRY GODMOTHER. And remember also how you are the best of them all!

The door closes by magic.

Enter CALLUM, *from the cupboard.*

CALLUM. Cinderella . . . She's gone. (*Sits by* THE BLACK DOUGLAS.) I wanted to ask her to stay, but why should she? There's nothing here to keep her.

FAIRY GODMOTHER (*surprised*). He is falling in love, I'm sure of it!

CALLUM (*angrily*). I used to dream of escape, but now I dream only of her! She is my prison now. (THE BLACK DOUGLAS *gives him a paw.*) You're a good friend . . . If only I knew what she thought of me.

FAIRY GODMOTHER. She will know you have a kind heart.

CALLUM. Come on, Douglas . . . She's gone, and there's work in the morning.

They go to cupboard.

FAIRY GODMOTHER. I wish I could help you, but I cannot –

Love is the secret that no-one can tell,
Not wizard nor witch, not fairy nor elf
For love is the secret that tells itself.

She withdraws into the darkness, and vanishes.

Scene Two

The ante-room to the ballroom. Music, and the sound of laughter and dancing from the ballroom.

Enter CLAUDINE *and* CLAUDETTE, *in their ballgowns, and in an evil temper.*

CLAUDINE. This is horrible!

CLAUDETTE. So it is! It's worse than horrible!

CLAUDINE. He's danced every dance . . .

CLAUDETTE. But he's danced them with that Princess Faraway!

CLAUDINE. He won't even look at us!

CLAUDETTE (*looking off, pointing*). And look at her – she's happy!

CLAUDETTE. The little witch! I'd like to push her down the stairs!

CLAUDINE. I'd like to bounce up and down on her head!

They bounce up and down venomously.

CLAUDETTE. We want The Prince!

CLAUDINE. So we should get The Prince!

CLAUDINE *and* CLAUDETTE (*in unison, still bouncing*). It's not fair! It's not fair! It's not fair!

Enter LADY CLAUDIA.

CLAUDIA. My little treasures, there, there. What's the matter?

CLAUDINE *and* CLAUDETTE (*in unison, hysterical*). HE'S
DANCING WITH HER! IT'S ALL GONE WRONG! IT'S
ALL GONE WRONG! IT'S ALL . . .

CLAUDIA. DON'T GET HYSTERICAL! (*She slaps*
CLAUDINE. CLAUDINE *slaps* CLAUDETTE.
CLAUDETTE *slaps* CLAUDIA, *who slaps* CLAUDINE
and CLAUDETTE *hard and in quick succession.*) DON'T
PANIC! Haven't you always got what you wanted? Well,
haven't you?

CLAUDINE *and* CLAUDETTE (*in unison, chastened a little*).
Yes, mama.

CLAUDIA. Look how we got rid of Isabella.

CLAUDINE. Oh yes, and turned her into stupid little
Cinderella.

CLAUDIA. Well, then! Never give up! We'll find a way.

CLAUDETTE. That's right – no-one's strong enough to beat
us.

CLAUDINE. If only they didn't look so good together.

CLAUDINE. They're coming this way!

CLAUDETTE. I can't look.

CLAUDIA. Then don't look, my lambs. Pretend it isn't
happening.

They look away, offended by the beauty and happiness of
CINDERELLA *and* PRINCE RUFUS *who enter, dancing. It
is as if they have left the ballroom to enjoy their dance in
private, to dance to the full.*

PRINCE. My princess . . . (*Takes her hand.*) You are afraid
that if I kiss your hand, I will kiss your arm, and if I kiss
your arm . . .

CINDERELLA *surprises him by leaning forward and
kissing him sweetly and passionately on the lips.*

CINDERELLA. I am not afraid.

They resume dancing as an admiring crowd gathers slowly from the ballroom. This includes KING JOHN *and* THE DANCING-BEAR.

The music ends. The PRINCE *bows to* CINDERELLA, *kisses her hand. The watching crowd applauds.* CLAUDIA, CLAUDINE *and* CLAUDETTE *are forced to join in the applause, for the look of the thing.*

PRINCE (*confidentially, to* CINDERELLA). I am the luckiest Prince who ever lived.

CINDERELLA. I never knew I could dance until I danced with you.

KING. How I love it when children behave the way they ought to behave.

CLAUDINE (*confidentially, to* CLAUDETTE). Look at her smiling and laughing, the little madam!

CLAUDETTE. I could strangle her with my bare hands!

CLAUDIA. Ssssh!

KING. It has made us all happy just watching you dance. I'm so happy I could dance with a bear.

He dances a few steps with the BEAR, *then presents him to* CINDERELLA. *The* BEAR *bows to her.*

PRINCE. See how he bows to you. He knows you are the loveliest of all. Do you like the bear?

CLAUDINE *and* CLAUDETTE *bite their hands, double up in agony.*

CINDERELLA (*stroking* BEAR). Oh yes, but it is he who is lovely. Only . . .

PRINCE. What is it?

CINDERELLA. He looks sad and lost in these clothes.

KING. It's his uniform. He is the royal dancing-bear.

CINDERELLA. You should let him run free.

KING. He is our pet and we must keep him.

CINDERELLA. Oh, but his sad eyes . . .

KING. That's my last word!

Enter SERGEANT PUFF *in his best dress uniform, and carrying the cake which has been beautifully iced. He seems lost and forlorn – he fails to see the crowd, and walks in the wrong direction.*

CLAUDIA. This way, Sergeant Puff!

He sees them, walks towards them, trips and nearly drops the cake.

CLAUDINE. Bungling fool!

CLAUDIA. The sergeant has baked one of his famous cakes. Well, sergeant – speak up.

PUFF. Me, Your Ladyship?

CLAUDIA. Yes, you!

PUFF (*painfully nervous*). Your majesty, lords, ladies and gentlemen, I'd say just to like . . . I'd just like to say . . . What an honour this is for me . . . To be here . . . And to give you this cake. (*Clears throat.*) Cooking is all I know, baking is what I do best . . .

CLAUDIA. Yes, yes – get on with it!

PUFF (*tailing off*). So please be so good as to eat it, and put it to the test.

CLAUDIA. That's enough, sergeant, thank you! (CLAUDINE *and* CLAUDETTE *snatch the cake greedily.*) You may go.

PUFF *goes to exit, wounded, feeling stupid.*

CLAUDINE (*greedily*). What a heavenly cake!

CLAUDETTE (*greedily*). I can taste it already!

CINDERELLA. Sergeant Puff. (*He stops.*) Before you go, I'd just like to say what a beautiful cake you have baked for us . . . I don't think any of us here really know how hard you must have worked . . . Thank you, sergeant Puff.

KING. Well spoken, Princess.

All applaud.

PUFF. You are very kind. (*He bows to* CINDERELLA.) Thank you.

He exits with great dignity.

KING. It is truly a most beautiful cake.

PRINCE. Then it must be given to the most beautiful of us all. (*Snatches cake from sisters, who are appalled.*) I offer it to you, Princess Faraway.

CINDERELLA. To me!

PRINCE. Please take the very first slice.

CINDERELLA. Oh no! I mean – no really, I couldn't!

PRINCE. But you must.

He gives cake to CINDERELLA.

CINDERELLA. I can't eat it! I can't eat it because . . . Because . . . I keep thinking of your poor little sister who can't come to the ball.

CLAUDINE. Our sister?

CLAUDETTE (*kicking* CLAUDINE). You know – the one we gave the oranges to.

CLAUDINE. Oh, her . . . I mean, the poor love. She loves cake even more than oranges.

CLAUDETTE. It's her favourite.

CINDERELLA. Then you must give the cake to her.

CLAUDINE *and* CLAUDETTE *snatch the cake.*

CLAUDINE. You're too kind.

CLAUDETTE. You've made someone very happy.

They exit with cake, their eyes sparkling with greed.

Music begins, from the ballroom.

KING. Any father would be proud to have you as his daughter. (*Bows to her.*)

CLAUDIA (*with an edge, taking his arm*). Come away, your majesty!

KING. Yes, come everyone! To the dance, to the dance!

He dances off with the BEAR. *Exeunt all save* THE PRINCE *and* CINDERELLA.

PRINCE. Stay, Princess Faraway. It is good to be alone.

CINDERELLA. I love to dance.

PRINCE. You will dance, and you will dance with no-one but me.

CINDERELLA. May I not even dance with the bear?

PRINCE. No, princess. Not even with him.

CINDERELLA. I must go soon.

PRINCE. I'll never let you go.

CINDERELLA. Then you will lose your princess.

PRINCE. How can that be? Must I let you go to keep you?

CINDERELLA. Yes, and if you keep me, you will lose me.

PRINCE. No, princess. I can't believe that . . . Come – I have gifts for you. Gifts of silver and gold.

CINDERELLA. To be here with you – that is gift enough for me.

PRINCE. Whatever you wish . . . We will dance again. We will dance The Midnight Waltz.

They begin to dance, enjoying The Midnight Waltz. A clock begins to strike twelve.

CINDERELLA. Midnight . . . Already? I have to go!

PRINCE. I won't let you go.

CINDERELLA. You don't understand – you've got to! (*She pulls free.*)

PRINCE. Come back, princess! Come back! (*He follows her, but* CLAUDINE *and* CLAUDETTE *enter and obstruct him.*) Stop her! Don't let her go! (*Enter* The DANCING-BEAR.) Princess Faraway! (*He breaks free of* CLAUDINE *and* CLAUDETTE, *but just as he is about to catch* CINDERELLA, *the* BEAR *takes him and dances with him.*)

CINDERELLA. I'm sorry, Prince. I would love to stay, but I can't. I'm sorry.

She exits, as CLAUDIA *enters.*

PRINCE. Princess Faraway . . . She's gone!

CLAUDIA. So now . . .

CLAUDINE *and* CLAUDETTE (*taking hold of* PRINCE, *in unison*). You can dance with us!

PRINCE. Never! (*Pulls away.*) If I can't dance with her I won't dance at all . . . Stop – stop the music! I command it! (*Music and dancing stops.*) Let there be no more dancing until she is here again. Lady Claudia.

CLAUDIA. Your Highness?

PRINCE. Tomorrow night you must give another ball – a grand ball.

CLAUDIA. It will be a pleasure, Prince Rufus.

PRINCE. She must come again . . . I am a Prince, I always get what I want! She will come again, and I will make her mine.

Exeunt all, save CLAUDIA, CLAUDINE *and* CLAUDETTE.

CLAUDIA (*delighted*). Another ball, my treasures – another chance to marry The Prince!

CLAUDINE *and* CLAUDETTE (*in unison*). We love you, mama.

Exit CLAUDINE.

CLAUDIA. Princess Faraway! (*Spits.*) She's no match for us.

CLAUDETTE. She's too stupid.

Enter CLAUDINE *with cake.*

CLAUDINE. She's so stupid she really thought we'd give this to Cinderella.

CLAUDIA. Quickly – cut it into three.

CLAUDINE (*cutting*). Oh yes – let's eat it all.

CLAUDETTE. So that no-one else gets any.

They snatch their portions, but just before they eat, they discover the AUDIENCE.

CLAUDIA (*to* AUDIENCE). You want some too, don't you?

AUDIENCE. No.

ALL. Oh yes you do!

AUDIENCE. Oh no we don't!

ALL. Oh yes you do!

AUDIENCE. Oh no we don't!

CLAUDETTE. You're just saying that.

CLAUDINE. Because you know we wouldn't give you any, anyway.

CLAUDIA. Right, my treasures – 1-2-3 and . . .

They guzzle the cake, groaning with pleasure.

CLAUDINE (*grimacing, mouth full*). Mine smells funny.

CLAUDETTE (*grimacing, mouth full*). So does mine.

CLAUDIA (*mouth full*). Don't be fussy – or I'll eat yours for you!

Exeunt, guzzling.

Scene Three

The castle kitchen. The next evening. CALLUM *carves his ring.* THE BLACK DOUGLAS *sits by the hearth.*

CALLUM. Look, Dougie . . . (*Shows ring to* THE BLACK DOUGLAS.) If I carve any more there'll be nothing left of it, and I won't have anything to give her at all.

Enter CINDERELLA, *working hard.*

CINDERELLA. It's all right for some! Where is everybody?

CALLUM (*quickly putting the ring away*). They've taken the food up to the grand ball.

CINDERELLA. A grand ball – I wonder what it will be like.

CALLUM. Never mind that. (*Eagerly.*) Tell me about last night again. Tell me about your sisters and the cake.

CINDERELLA. I asked my sisters to give the cake to poor little Cinderella, but I knew they would give it to themselves.

CALLUM (*laughing*). I bet they ate it all.

CINDERELLA (*laughing*). I bet they did – every last piece.

CALLUM. It serves them right. I wish I could have seen them eat it.

CINDERELLA. I can see them in my mind's eye.

She imitates the sisters guzzling.

CALLUM (*laughing*). Yes, or like this.

He imitates the sisters guzzling.

CINDERELLA (*laughing*). Or like this.

She imitates the sisters guzzling.

Enter SERGEANT PUFF.

PUFF. What are you laughing at, the pair of you?

CINDERELLA *and* CALLUM (*still laughing, in unison*). Nothing.

PUFF. You've done nothing but laugh all day.

CINDERELLA. You should try it.

PUFF. That'll be the day. (THE BLACK DOUGLAS *barks.*) What are you wanting, furface? (THE BLACK DOUGLAS *sits and stares intensely at him.*) I'm dead tired – another royal ball tonight! But I wonder if she'll be there.

CALLUM. She? Who's she?

PUFF. Oh you should have seen her . . . (*To* THE BLACK DOUGLAS.) Stop staring at me like that! (*Dog keeps staring.* PUFF *continues.*) Even though I was just a poor sergeant and she was a princess, she came right up to me and thanked me for all my work . . . I'll never forget it, never in the rest of . . . Will you stop staring! He's making me feel guilty.

He keeps staring at Puff.

CALLUM (*teasingly*). I'd like to meet this princess.

PUFF. You meet her? Don't be daft. (CINDERELLA *sticks her tongue out at* CALLUM. THE BLACK DOUGLAS *barks, continues to stare.*) Shut it, Furface!

CINDERELLA. It's like he's trying to remind you of something.

PUFF. Don't be ridiculous . . . You're right! His tea! I've forgotten to give him his tea! (THE BLACK DOUGLAS *barks in agreement.*) I'm sorry, Douglas. I've been too busy making food for everyone else. Come on, and we'll get you fed. Come on, you useless big lump.

Exeunt PUFF *and* THE BLACK DOUGLAS.

CALLUM. He's a kind man . . . I'll miss him.

CINDERELLA. You'll miss him?

CALLUM. Yes – I'm going to break out of here.

CINDERELLA. You can't . . . I mean, there are guards at the gates.

CALLUM. Then I'll fight them. I won't be a prisoner any more!

He takes the ring out, unseen by CINDERELLA.

CINDERELLA. Please don't go . . . It would be horrible here without you.

CALLUM. Then come with me.

CINDERELLA. Come with you! I couldn't.

CALLUM. Yes you could! We'll get past the guards while the guests are arriving. We'll take The Great North Road to the mountains. (*Takes her hand.*) Come with me!

CINDERELLA (*pulling back*). This is my home . . . and there is The Prince . . .

CALLUM. Come on!

CINDERELLA. I couldn't . . . I don't know . . . (*A horrid babbling sound is heard from off.*) Listen.

CALLUM. Your sisters! (*Puts the ring away.*) Trust them!

Enter CLAUDINE *and* CLAUDETTE.

CLAUDINE *and* CLAUDETTE (*in unison*). Guess who!

CLAUDETTE. We just had to show you what we're wearing for the grand ball.

CLAUDINE. Poor Cinderella.

CLAUDETTE. We know how much you want to come.

CLAUDINE. Shame you're going to be disappointed!

They laugh loudly.

CLAUDETTE. And there's something else – one of us is going to marry The Prince.

CLAUDINE. Mama said so.

CINDERELLA. That's not what I've heard.

CLAUDINE *and* CLAUDETTE (*outraged, in unison*). What did you say?

CINDERELLA. I've heard that a princess has come to the ball – the Princess Faraway! The Prince has fallen in love with her, and he'll marry her, not you or you – that's what I've heard!

CALLUM *hangs his head, hurt.*

CLAUDINE *and* CLAUDETTE (*in unison*). Who told you that?

CINDERELLA. It's all over the castle.

CLAUDINE. We'll get you for that!

CLAUDETTE. We'll break every bone in your body!

CALLUM. Leave her alone!

CINDERELLA. It's all right, Callum. I'm not scared of them. There's nothing they can do to hurt me any more!

Enter SERGEANT PUFF *and* THE BLACK DOUGLAS.

PUFF. His tea went down without touching the sides . . . Oh no!

CLAUDINE. What's that dog doing in the kitchen?

PUFF (*trying to hide him*). What dog?

CLAUDETTE. That dog! You can't hide him from us.

CLAUDINE (*shouting off*). Mama, Mama – come quickly.

CINDERELLA. Why can't you leave us alone?

PUFF. He's not doing any harm.

CLAUDETTE. Dogs are not allowed! Are they, Claudine?

CLAUDINE. Certainly not, Claudette. Mama, Mama!

CLAUDETTE. Oh, we'll hurt you all right!

Enter CLAUDIA.

CLAUDIA. You called, my treasures.

CLAUDINE *and* CLAUDETTE (*in unison, pointing*). Look, Mama!

CLAUDIA (*screams*). A dog – I hate dogs! Get him away from me!

PUFF. He's very friendly, Your Importance . . .

CLAUDIA. I WILL NOT TOLERATE THAT STINKING BRUTE IN MY CASTLE!

CINDERELLA. But he's the only fun we ever have.

CLAUDIA. FUN? YOU'RE NOT HERE TO HAVE FUN! SERGEANT PUFF – TAKE HIM OUT INTO THE WOODS AND MAKE SURE HE NEVER COMES BACK!

CALLUM. Never . . . You mean . . . ?

CLAUDIA. Exactly.

CINDERELLA. But you can't! (*To* AUDIENCE.) She can't kill The Black Douglas, can she?

AUDIENCE. No!

CLAUDIA, CLAUDINE *and* CLAUDETTE (*all together*). Oh yes she can!

AUDIENCE. Oh no she can't!

CLAUDIA (*to* AUDIENCE). THAT'S WHERE YOU'RE WRONG! TAKE HIM AWAY, SERGEANT – FOREVER! (*Hands* PUFF *a large kitchen cleaver.*) THAT'S AN ORDER.

CALLUM. Please, Sergeant Puff – don't do it . . .

PUFF (*sternly*). I have been given an order.

CLAUDIA. And he never disobeys an order!

CALLUM. Sergeant Puff . . . Please . . .

PUFF (*sadly, to* THE BLACK DOUGLAS). Here, boy. Good boy. Come on now.

Exits, followed trustingly by THE BLACK DOUGLAS.

CLAUDINE *and* CLAUDETTE (*in unison*). Ha, ha, ha!

CLAUDIA. You can't keep a secret from us!

CALLUM (*in a violent rage*). GET OUT OF HERE!

CLAUDIA. DON'T YOU DARE TALK TO . . .

CALLUM. I SAID – GET OUT!

CLAUDINE. Run, Mama!

CLAUDETTE. He's gone wild!

CALLUM. GO ON – LEAVE US ALONE! (*Exeunt* CLAUDIA, CLAUDINE *and* CLAUDETTE, *at a run.*) I hate them. I hate them all!

CINDERELLA. They take everything!

CALLUM. I can't stay here! I will ask you one more time . . .

CINDERELLA. Please, don't . . .

CALLUM. Come with me, come with me out into the world.

CINDERELLA. Why must you ask? I'm sorry about The Black Douglas . . . Don't make me come.

CALLUM. If you come with me, you must come of your own free will. I would never force you!

CINDERELLA. I know you wouldn't.

CALLUM. Then give me your answer.

CINDERELLA. I wish I could . . . Help me, magic – help me.

CALLUM (*bitterly*). Magic! (THE FAIRY GODMOTHER *appears.*) What magic is there here?

FAIRY GODMOTHER. Tell me your wish and I will help you.

CINDERELLA. I don't know what I wish.

FAIRY GODMOTHER. Then you must help yourself.

Music from the ball begins, and can be heard in the distance.

CALLUM. Listen.

CINDERELLA. The music! I must see The Prince again . . . I never knew I could dance until I danced with him . . . I'm sorry, Callum . . . I must go to The Prince.

CALLUM. Goodbye, Cinderella.

CINDERELLA. Goodbye?

CALLUM. You have given me your answer.

CINDERELLA. Goodbye, Callum . . . (*He exits to cupboard.*) I couldn't bear not to see The Prince again.

FAIRY GODMOTHER. Go on your way. (*She gestures, the door opens by magic.*) The tree will dress you . . . You will be the most beautiful of them all.

CINDERELLA. I don't feel beautiful . . . I'm sorry, Callum . . . but listen to the music!

She exits at a run.

FAIRY GODMOTHER. May love tell you its secret.

The door closes by magic.

Enter CALLUM, *with his bundle.*

CALLUM. They've taken The Black Douglas and now I've lost her . . . Princess Faraway . . . She said it herself – she will marry The Prince. (*Slings bundle over his shoulder.*) Then I will go alone! I will fight the guards and I will be free!

THE FAIRY GODMOTHER *gestures, the door opens by magic.* CALLUM *goes to exit.*

FAIRY GODMOTHER. He will not go . . . He loves her . . . He cannot go.

CALLUM *stops.*

CALLUM (*angry*). Why can't I leave here? (*Flings down bundle.*) What is there to keep me?

FAIRY GODMOTHER. He has hope in his heart.

CALLUM. I am a fool to wait! There is nothing here!

FAIRY GODMOTHER.
Try out your love, test its magic power,
Give your princess till the midnight hour.

CALLUM. I will give her till midnight.

FAIRY GODMOTHER (*to* AUDIENCE). Till midnight!

Scene Four

The ante-room to the ballroom. Music and the sound of laughter and dancing from the ballroom.

Enter KING *and* THE PRINCE.

PRINCE. She's here, father! She has come again.

KING. I am glad for you.

PRINCE. She is more beautiful than ever . . . Her eyes sparkle like diamonds!

KING. Have a care – she has a magic about her. She may escape you yet.

PRINCE. Never . . . I have posted a guard beyond the door.

KING. This is no way to keep her!

PRINCE. I will not lose her again!

Enter CLAUDIA, CLAUDINE *and* CLAUDETTE, *scheming amongst themselves.*

CLAUDIA. I will engage her in conversation – you do the rest.

CLAUDINE *and* CLAUDETTE (*in unison*). Yes, Mama.

CINDERELLA enters with THE DANCING-BEAR, *unseen by* CLAUDIA, CLAUDINE *and* CLAUDETTE.

PRINCE. My Princess!

CLAUDINE *and* CLAUDETTE *throw their arms wide in delight.*

CLAUDINE *and* CLAUDETTE (*in unison*). My Prince!

THE PRINCE *rushes past them, to* CINDERELLA.

PRINCE. How do you like The Grand Ball?

CINDERELLA. It is always so grand here.

PRINCE. It has been held in your honour . . . Wait here. I have gifts for you . . . Come, father.

Exeunt THE PRINCE *and* KING. CLAUDIA *'engages'* CINDERELLA.

CLAUDIA. My, my – aren't we looking well tonight.

CINDERELLA. How very kind of you to say so.

Unseen by CINDERELLA, CLAUDINE *and* CLAUDETTE *produce vicious looking clubs from behind their backs, and approach* CINDERELLA *menacingly.*

CLAUDIA. And isn't it fine weather for this time of year?

CINDERELLA. Is it?

CLAUDIA. Oh yes, Princess, very fine . . . A little changeable perhaps! (*But* CLAUDINE *and* CLAUDETTE *are stared out by the* BEAR, *and are forced to hide their clubs as* THE PRINCE *and the* KING *enter carrying a huge caske*t.) Fools!

PRINCE. For you, Princess Faraway. (*Throws open the casket.*) The Royal Jewels! Choose – you may take whatever you wish. (CLAUDIA, CLAUDINE *and* CLAUDETTE *sink to their knees in adoration.* CINDERELLA *turns away from the casket.*) Well, then – what would you like?

CINDERELLA. Nothing.

KING. Nothing?

PRINCE. What can this mean?

CINDERELLA. Forgive me, Prince, but you give me too much.

PRINCE. You can never have too much . . . My ships will bring you more oranges than you can dream of . . . Each day you will sleep on a bed as soft as air, and we will dance at a ball every night of the year.

CINDERELLA. Every night?

PRINCE. I will marry you, and one day you will be my queen.

CLAUDINE *and* CLAUDETTE *hug each other, and sob.*

KING (*clapping*). There – it is settled!

CINDERELLA. No! Nothing is settled! You have not asked me.

PRINCE. I do not ask because I know you will not refuse me.

CINDERELLA. I will make up my own mind! You must give me time.

PRINCE. Time! Tell me – is there another?

CINDERELLA (*thinking it for the first time*). There is someone . . . Someone who would not force me.

PRINCE. Then he does not love you as I do!

CINDERELLA. It may be he loves me more.

PRINCE. Impossible! I would do anything for you.

CINDERELLA. Anything? Then let me go from here.

PRINCE. Anything but that . . . Music! I want loud music! (*Music begins.*) Come, Princess – The Midnight Waltz. This time we will dance it together . . . Everybody, dance! I command it!

Everybody dances. CINDERELLA *dances with the* BEAR.

CINDERELLA. You shall not keep me here!

She breaks free of the dancers and runs to the door, but THE PRINCE *blocks her path.*

PRINCE. Not this time, my Princess! There is no escape!

CINDERELLA *turns and runs into the ballroom.*

PRINCE. Catch her! Catch her!

Exeunt all in pursuit, save CLAUDIA, CLAUDINE, CLAUDETTE *and the* BEAR.

CLAUDIA. At last – this is our chance!

CLAUDINE. If we find her first . . .

CLAUDETTE (*slapping club into her palm*). No more sweet little princess!

CLAUDIA. After her!

Exeunt CLAUDIA, CLAUDINE *and* CLAUDETTE, *at a run.*

The BEAR *dances The Midnight Waltz briefly on his own, and gathers* CINDERELLA *into his arms as she enters at a run.*

CINDERELLA. They're right behind me! Hide me, Bear. Please hide me!

The BEAR *hides her behind his back. Enter* THE PRINCE *and other* GUESTS.

PRINCE. That way – the dining-hall . . . Search under every table! Find her! Catch her!

Exeunt THE PRINCE *and other* GUESTS.

CINDERELLA. Thank you, Bear . . . (*Goes to door.*) This is the only way out. (*Opens door – her way is blocked by a terrifying* GUARD, *armed with an axe.*) There's a guard! I'll never be free!

She runs back to the BEAR, *who hides her again as* CLAUDINE *and* CLAUDETTE *enter at a run.*

CLAUDINE. We've got to find her first!

CLAUDETTE. The little witch – I can't wait!

Exeunt CLAUDINE *and* CLAUDETTE.

CINDERELLA. But where can I go – there is no way out!

She runs – straight into the arms of her FATHER.

FATHER. Got you!

CINDERELLA. The Lord-General!

FATHER. I've been watching you from my little corner.

CINDERELLA. I'll never escape.

FATHER. It is wrong of him to trap you like an animal.

CINDERELLA. Then you will help me?

FATHER. You remind me of my own dear daughter . . . She used to be sweet and gentle, but now she's wild and cheeky.

CINDERELLA. My own dear father – he used to be clever and strong, but now he's old and stupid.

FATHER. I hope I never hear my daughter talk like that about me. (*Midnight begins to strike.*)

CINDERELLA. Midnight! The magic runs out.

FATHER. Hurry – I will help you.

CINDERELLA (*losing a shoe*). My shoe . . .

FATHER. Leave it! (*He pulls back a wall hanging.*) Behind here . . . I'll lead them away from you – it's all I can do. (*She hides behind the wall hanging. Enter* THE PRINCE, *and* GUESTS.) That way, Your Highness! I'm sure I saw her. (*He exits.*)

PRINCE. Follow him! She is mine! She must be mine! Hurry!

Exeunt THE PRINCE, *and* GUESTS.

Enter CLAUDIA, *snooping. She opens the casket hungrily, and is disappointed not to find* PRINCESS FARAWAY. *There are movements from behind the hanging. The* BEAR *tries to hide them, but* CLAUDIA *glares at him suspiciously.*

CLAUDIA. I know a guilty bear when I see one! Out of my way, brute! (*Pushes* BEAR *aside, sees movement behind hanging.*) Aha! I have her!

She gets behind hanging and makes her way clumsily towards CINDERELLA.

Enter CLAUDINE *and* CLAUDETTE. *The* BEAR *exaggerates his attempts to mask the hanging.*

CLAUDINE. She is a witch – she's vanished!

CLAUDETTE. But wait – look at the bear!

CLAUDINE. He's hiding something. There – look!

CLAUDINE. We've found her!

CLAUDETTE. Right then – 1-2-3 and . . .

They deliver great swinging blows with their clubs to the struggling shape trapped behind the hanging.

CLAUDINE. I love this!

CLAUDETTE. Mama will be so pleased!

CLAUDIA, *bruised and battered, emerges from behind the hanging.*

CLAUDIA. It's me, you fools!

CLAUDINE *and* CLAUDETTE (*in unison*). Mama!

CLAUDIA *grabs them by their throats, shakes them.*

CLAUDIA. Can't you do anything right? (*The clock has stopped striking.* CLAUDIA *points at the hanging.*) That's her – There, there! Bring her to me!

CLAUDINE *and* CLAUDETTE *pull back the hanging to reveal* CINDERELLA, *once more in her ragged clothes.*

CLAUDINE *and* CLAUDETTE (*in unison*). Cinderella!

CLAUDIA. And just what do you think you're doing here?

CINDERELLA. I . . . I was jealous. I wanted to see everything at the ball, all the clothes and the music . . .

CLAUDIA. How dare you creep in here! Guard – let her pass! (To CINDERELLA.) YOU FILTHY LITTLE GIRL – GET BACK TO THE KITCHEN WHERE YOU BELONG!

CINDERELLA (*curtseying*). Yes, Lady Claudia.

CLAUDIA (*to* CLAUDINE *and* CLAUDETTE). Find the princess!

They continue their search.

CINDERELLA (*to herself*). How strange – Cinderella has set
me free. (*The* BEAR *bows to her and she kisses him.*)
Thank you, Bear. (*She exits at a run, past the GUARD.*)

Enter THE PRINCE, KING *and* GUESTS.

PRINCE. Who has passed through the door?

CLAUDIA. It was nobody, Your Highness.

CLAUDINE. Only a dirty little kitchen girl.

KING. A kitchen girl?

PRINCE. My Princess has escaped me again – how can it be?

KING. She had a magic about her. You must let her go . . .

PRINCE. Her shoe! (*Picks it up, cherishes it.*) Her glass shoe.

KING. Give her up, my son . . .

PRINCE. I will use the shoe to find her . . . Search the castle!
Whoever fits the shoe will be my bride – I swear it!

KING. And I tell you to leave it be!

PRINCE. Search the castle!

Exeunt THE PRINCE *and* GUESTS.

CLAUDIA (*to* CLAUDINE *and* CLAUDETTE). One of you
must fit the shoe!

CLAUDETTE. But our feet are too big!

CLAUDIA. We'll soon see to that! Come with me.

Exeunt CLAUDIA, CLAUDINE *and* CLAUDETTE.

KING. Come back, I tell you! Come back . . . I give up – he
must learn what he learns. (*Wearily, to* BEAR.) So it's you
and me, old Dancer . . . It's true what she said – you have
sad eyes. Come – dance for me one more time, and I will
take you down to the castle gates and let you run free.

Exeunt KING *and* BEAR, *dancing.*

Scene Five

The castle kitchen.

Enter CINDERELLA.

CINDERELLA. Dark and dirty old kitchen – I never thought
I would be glad to see you, but I am . . . I am. (*Runs to
cupboard.*) I've come back. (*Knocks on door.*) Wake up,
wake up . . . Please be here, please . . . (*Opens door.*)
He's gone.

Enter CALLUM, *from the shadows.*

CALLUM. I've waited and waited and waited.

CINDERELLA. You're still here! I was frightened you had
gone away and left me.

CALLUM. And I was frightened you would go to the ball and
never come back.

CALLUM *and* CINDERELLA (*together*). I . . .

CALLUM. You first.

CINDERELLA. No, you first.

CALLUM (*taking out ring*). This ring – I've carved it for
you . . . Only for you . . . I'd like to . . .

Enter SERGEANT PUFF, *dejected.*

CINDERELLA. Sergeant Puff!

PUFF. Are you two still up?

CINDERELLA. What's the matter, Sergeant Puff?

PUFF. I couldn't sleep . . . I've never felt so miserable.

CINDERELLA. The poor Black Douglas.

CALLUM. He was the best dog in the world, and now he's
gone.

PUFF. What? No, no – it's not that.

CINDERELLA. What is it, then?

PUFF. For the first time in my life I have disobeyed an order.

CALLUM. Disobeyed?

CINDERELLA. You mean . . .

PUFF. Aye . . . (*Whistles.*)

Enter THE BLACK DOUGLAS.

CALLUM *and* CINDERELLA (*together*). The Black Douglas!

They hug and pat THE BLACK DOUGLAS.

CINDERELLA. Oh, it's good to see you, Dougie!

CALLUM. I thought you were gone forever! Thank you, Sergeant Puff.

PUFF *sits down, utterly dejected.*

CINDERELLA. Don't be so sad.

CALLUM. You should be proud of yourself.

PUFF. Me – disobey an order? I'm ashamed of myself.

CINDERELLA. If only we could make him laugh.

CALLUM. It's impossible.

CINDERELLA. I wonder . . . Sergeant Puff?

PUFF (*gruffly*). What is it?

CINDERELLA. You know when we mixed the icing for your cake? Well, The Black Douglas, he . . .

CALLUM. You can't tell him that!

CINDERELLA. I'm going to . . . He came right up to the mixing-bowl and he, he . . .

THE BLACK DOUGLAS *mimes his despicable deed.*

CINDERELLA. He did that right in the icing mixture!

PUFF (*furious*). HE DID WHAT!

CINDERELLA. And we stirred it in!

PUFF. YOU MEAN TO TELL ME HE DID THAT IN MY BEAUTIFUL CAKE?

CINDERELLA. Yes.

PUFF. AND I GAVE IT TO ALL THE GRAND PEOPLE AT THE BALL?

CINDERELLA. Yes.

PUFF. THIS IS TERRIBLE, TERRIBLE! I DON'T BELIEVE IT, I DON'T . . . (*A little laughter escapes.*)

CALLUM (*amazed*). It's working!

PUFF (*trying to stay furious*). NOTHING'S WORKING, YOU LITTLE MONKEYS! I'M TELLING YOU THIS IS THE . . . THIS IS THE . . . (*Begins to laugh.*) FUNNIEST THING I'VE EVER HEARD IN MY WHOLE LIFE! (PUFF *laughs and laughs and laughs.* CALLUM *and* CINDERELLA *clap and laugh with joy.*) OH, IT HURTS . . . AND ME IN MY BEST UNIFORM . . . IT HURTS . . .

CALLUM. You've done it! You've made him laugh!

CINDERELLA (*to* PUFF). And my sisters ate it!

PUFF (*laughing all the more*). Oh-ho-ho! It couldn't be better . . .

A horrid babbling from off.

CINDERELLA. Someone's coming!

CALLUM. Quickly, Dougie – hide! (*Exit* THE BLACK DOUGLAS.)

Enter CLAUDIA, CLAUDINE *and* CLAUDETTE, *at a run.*

CLAUDIA. I need two hammers – quickly!

PUFF *points at sisters, and laughs.*

CLAUDINE. He's laughing!

CLAUDIA. Never mind him! Quickly – the hammers.

PUFF. Two hammers, Your Importance. Here you are.

He gives hammers to CLAUDIA.

CLAUDIA. Perfect! (*To her daughters.*) We must make your feet a little smaller.

CLAUDINE *and* CLAUDETTE (*in unison*). Mama?

CLAUDIA *gives them a hammer each.*

CLAUDIA. You bash her foot, and she'll bash yours!

CLAUDINE *and* CLAUDETTE (*in unison*). But my poor foot!

CLAUDIA. What will you need feet for if you're a princess? You'll have others to do your walking! Get on with it!

CLAUDINE *and* CLAUDETTE (*in unison*). But Mama!!!!!

CLAUDIA. DO WHAT YOU'RE TOLD! (*They commence bashing each other's foot, screaming with pain but driven on by thoughts of* THE PRINCE *and of the agony they must be causing each other.*) THAT'S IT! THAT'S MY GIRLS. HARDER! HARDER! HURRY – THE PRINCE IS COMING!

CINDERELLA. The Prince! (*She shrinks into the shadows.*)

Enter THE PRINCE, FATHER *and* GUESTS.

PRINCE. What a horrible place! I'll never find my princess here.

FATHER. We have searched everywhere else.

CLAUDIA. Your Highness – you did say you would marry whoever can fit the shoe?

PRINCE. I gave my word.

CLAUDIA (*snatching shoe*). One of you, quickly – try it on!

> CLAUDETTE *gets there first, after a struggle with* CLAUDINE. CLAUDIA *fits the shoe on her foot.*

CLAUDIA (*crazed with delight*). It fits!

PRINCE (*appalled*). Then I must marry her!

CLAUDINE. No!

> Look there, the blood – it shows,
> The little cheat, she's bashed her toes!

> Fit it on me, mama! (CLAUDIA *fits the shoe on her foot.*)

CLAUDIA. It fits!

CLAUDETTE. No!

> There, the blood – look and see
> She's as big a cheat as me!

> If I can't have him, neither can you! (CLAUDINE *and* CLAUDETTE *begin to fight.*)

FATHER. STOP THAT IMMEDIATELY!

The fighting stops.

CALLUM. I can show you your princess.

PRINCE (*disbelieving*). You can? My princess wears silk and lace.

CALLUM. My princess wears rags.

PRINCE. Mine has shoes of glass.

CALLUM. My princess goes barefoot.

PRINCE. Mine has hair as smooth as gold.

CALLUM. My princess's hair is all in tangles.

He pulls CINDERELLA *out of the shadows.*

PRINCE. It's not her . . . She's a kitchen girl . . . It can't be her!

CALLUM *takes the shoe. He kneels by* CINDERELLA, *and fits the shoe.*

ALL. It fits!

GUESTS. You!

CLAUDINE *and* CLAUDETTE. You!

CLAUDIA. You!

PUFF. You!

FATHER. You!

PRINCE (*quietly*). It is you!

CINDERELLA (*quietly*). Hullo, Prince.

CLAUDINE *and* CLAUDETTE (*in unison*). Cinderella?

CALLUM. No! She's not Cinderella any more – she's Isabella again.

ISABELLA (*savouring the thought*). Oh yes – Isabella again . . .

PRINCE. I've found you! You shall still be mine. I know I shouldn't have tried to keep you . . . (ISABELLA *takes* CALLUM's *hand.*) . . . I've lost you, haven't I? I do not deserve you, for I did not know you in these ragged clothes . . . I will not make that mistake again. Let me kiss your hand. (*Kisses her hand.*) Goodbye, Princess.

ISABELLA. Goodbye, Prince.

PRINCE (*bows to her*). May you be happy.

Exeunt THE PRINCE *and* GUESTS.

FATHER. What's been going on here?

CLAUDIA (*tearful*). Please forgive me, dear husband . . . You mustn't be angry with me . . .

FATHER. STOP YOUR TEARS! NO-ONE BELIEVES THEM! IT'S ALL JUST A STUPID ACT!

CLAUDIA (*recovering immediately*). Yes, you're quite right! I've always lied and cheated . . . I'm a stupid, stupid woman. Isabella . . . what can I say? We've robbed you and tricked you and tormented you, we've called you Cinderella and laughed at you, but you've beaten us all the same . . . See how happy you are! I congratulate you – you are stronger than I thought possible.

CLAUDINE *and* CLAUDETTE (*in unison, confused*). Mama?

CLAUDIA. KEEP QUIET, THE PAIR OF YOU! LOOK AT YOU! YOU'VE HAD EVERYTHING YOU EVER WANTED, AND LOOK WHAT YOU'VE GOT – NOTHING! I wonder . . . If Isabella can learn so much in Puff's kitchen . . . That's it! (*To* CLAUDINE *and* CLAUDETTE.) YOU WILL LIVE AND WORK IN THE KITCHEN UNTIL YOU LEARN YOUR LESSON!

CLAUDINE *and* CLAUDETTE (*in unison*). We don't want to learn our lesson!

CLAUDIA. YOU'LL DO WHAT YOU'RE TOLD!

CLAUDINE. It wasn't just us!

CLAUDETTE. What about you?

CLAUDIA. ME, ME? I'VE GOT TO BE ME EVERY DAY FOR THE REST OF MY LIFE! WHAT COULD BE WORSE THAN THAT? WHAT COULD POSSIBLY BE WORSE THAN THAT? (*Exits, in a state.*)

CLAUDINE *and* CLAUDETTE (*in unison, running after her*). Mama – don't leave us here!

FATHER. YOU HEARD WHAT SHE SAID – IT'S THE KITCHEN FOR YOU! (*They make a run for it.*) Stop them, Sergeant! (PUFF *grabs them, hauls them to the cupboard.*)

CLAUDINE *and* CLAUDETTE (*in unison*). It's not fair, it's not fair, it's not fair!

FATHER. IT'S PERFECTLY FAIR!

PUFF (*opens door to cupboard*). You even have your own bedroom!

CALLUM *takes* CINDERELLA's *hand, and they leave, unseen by the others.*

CLAUDINE *and* CLAUDETTE (*in unison*) No, no – this is horrible!

FATHER *and* PUFF *push them into the cupboard, slam the door, lock it.*

PUFF. And work starts before it's light!

FATHER. Now, Isabella – I want to talk to you.

PUFF. Excuse me, sir . . .

FATHER. Be quiet, Sergeant Puff . . . I've been wrong, Isabella . . .

PUFF. She's not here, sir.

FATHER. Not here? Why didn't you tell me? I have to talk to her, I have to . . .

Exeunt FATHER, *followed by* PUFF. THE FAIRY GOD-MOTHER *appears, by magic. She picks up the glass shoe.*

FAIRY GODMOTHER.
Love's secret is out, but before you go free,
Come to the tree, Isabella, to the tree and to me.

She places the shoe on the fire. It explodes with a magical light, and the kitchen is transformed to the opening scene – the tree and the grave by the castle gates. THE FAIRY GODMOTHER *stands under the branches of the tree.*

Enter ISABELLA *and* CALLUM.

CALLUM (*gazing at the gates*). The gates! How high they are!

ISABELLA. My little tree . . .

FAIRY GODMOTHER.
I'm sure I know
I'm sure I'm right

He's the wish
You wished tonight.

ISABELLA. Oh yes, he is!

Thank you, my little tree
For all you have given to me.

FAIRY GODMOTHER. I must give you this . . . (*She produces a beautiful coat from the branches of the tree, gives it to her.*) It is for your journey.

ISABELLA. Callum, look what the tree has given me! (*She puts it on.*) It's beautiful! (*To tree.*) I will never forget you.

FAIRY GODMOTHER. Then you will never be forgotten. (*Vanishes.*)

CALLUM (*pointing*). Your father!

ISABELLA. We must go . . .

CALLUM. But the gates!

Enter FATHER *and* SERGEANT PUFF.

FATHER. Wait!

CALLUM. Don't try to stop us!

FATHER. I won't stop you . . . Isabella, do you wish to go with this boy?

ISABELLA. Yes, father – I do.

FATHER. Then I will not keep you here . . . He has cared for you better than I. (*To* CALLUM.) Here – take my coat. It is for your journey. (*Throws him his coat.*) May we live in peace.

CALLUM (*slings coat over his shoulder*). I will see that we do.

FATHER (*thunderous*). Open the gates!

The gates swing slowly open. A bright, full moon shines down on The Great North Road which stretches into the distance.

ISABELLA. Thank you, father. (*Hugs him.*)

FATHER. Will you come back and see me one day?

ISABELLA. I will.

FATHER. Goodbye, Isabella . . . (*Exits.*)

ISABELLA. Goodbye, father . . .

CALLUM. Here we go, Isabella – out into the world!

ISABELLA (*joyful*). Out into the world! (*Kisses* CALLUM.)

CALLUM. I've carved you this ring. I'd like to . . .

ISABELLA (*impatient, kind*). Oh . . . (*She takes ring, puts it on her finger.*) There . . . (*Kisses ring.*) It is done.

CALLUM. Come on, then. (*Turns back to* SERGEANT PUFF) Sergeant Puff, won't you come with us?

PUFF. And leave my kitchen? No, I'll stay where I am. (*Whistles.*)

ISABELLA. Of course – The Black Douglas!

CALLUM. How could we forget? (THE BLACK DOUGLAS *enters and runs to* PUFF's *side.*) Come on, Dougie.

THE BLACK DOUGLAS *stands between* PUFF *and* CALLUM *and* ISABELLA, *in two minds.*

PUFF. On you go, Furface. (*Pats* THE BLACK DOUGLAS.) You're a good dog, but you're better off with them . . . On you go . . . (THE BLACK DOUGLAS *runs to them.*)

CALLUM *and* ISABELLA (*in unison*). Goodbye, Sergeant Puff.

PUFF. Goodbye, Furface . . . Goodbye, Callum . . . Goodbye, Isabella. (*Exits.*)

CALLUM *and* ISABELLA (*in unison, to* AUDIENCE). Goodbye everyone.

CALLUM *and* ISABELLA, *together of course with* THE BLACK DOUGLAS, *turn and walk through the castle gates, which close slowly behind them.*

End.

Afterword

Children know more than adults – when they grow up they forget. Children know more because they think with their instinct not their reason. They carry the burden of what awaits them. Krysztof Kieslowski

When I was four I was taken into hospital for an eye operation. But no-one had told me the full story. My parents, through misguided kindness, had not told me I would have to stay in, and hoped to steal away with as little fuss as possible. Suddenly they were waving at me through a window, and they were gone! My stomach lurched, fireworks exploded in front of my eyes, and there was a roaring sound in my ears. I was abandoned, alone! I barely managed to hold back the tears, and so began the whole ridiculous struggle to be brave. The seven-year-old girl who shared the ward with me seemed impossibly pretty and grown-up. And then there was the nurse! This severe and intolerant woman took an instant dislike to me. I imagined that my mother had insisted too forcibly that she be kind to me and thus had poisoned her irretrievably against me. The nurse took away my toys on the grounds that they were unhygienic. Together the seven-year-old girl and I stood against her and when she disappeared the next day we felt we had won a great and magical victory.

Years later, when a teacher read out the story of *Hansel and Gretel*, I felt dizzy, as if someone had spied on my dreams. This fairy-tale could not simply be a story. This, clearly, was the truth.

I think I understood then that good stories tell the truth about how difficult life can be, and therefore now when I write a play for children I try to satisfy their craving for seriousness every bit as much as their craving for fun and nonsense.

I have been lucky enough to see many excellent and bewilderingly different productions of my plays for children.

The best of them have been distinguished by directors, actors, designers and composers who can view seriousness and nonsense as more or less equal partners. (I may take fairy-tales seriously but there can be few pleasures as enjoyable as watching a dour Scottish actor climb inside a furry suit.) But there have also been some bad productions and the worst of these invariably mistake worthiness for seriousness, goodie-goodie cuteness for courage and knowingness for nonsense – a deadly, depressing mix.

A large family audience wants and deserves a more genuine and powerful form of dramatic story-telling than it usually gets from pantomime. And yet there is much to be learned from the music-hall bravado of panto, and I try to be true to what I understand as the magic of fairy tales without losing any of the energy, vulgarity and mischief of good panto. If there's an equation it's this – taking the story seriously, telling it clearly, and asking the audience to believe in it equals far more fun. An audience only really laughs when it cares about the story.

An attempt to achieve this balance in the theatre tends to correspond with the balance already present in fairy-tales. The 'Cinderella' story, for instance, tells us many important truths – that life is often cruelly hard, but if we hang on to our better instincts a happy future is possible; that the love of a parent for its child (presented in the shape of the graveside tree and the ancient hearth) does indeed have the power to transform the world; that the longed-for triumph of good over evil is far from automatic and must be striven for; that inner freedom affords the key to our courage and identity. And yet, while we may need the story for its ability to remind us of these, and many other truths, we love it for its romance, its mischief, and its magic. In writing my play *Cinderella* it was as important to have the dog pee in Puff's cake as it was to replace the familiar pumpkin-coach with the older and far more beautiful image of the graveside tree. To me this kind of robust vulgarity is true to the spirit of the tale, for *Cinderella*, like all fairy-tales, belongs to the folk. It often feels that these great stories have crawled out of the swamp with us, fulfilling what Tolkien described as 'the imaginative satisfaction of ancient desires' and it's as if we have all miraculously had a hand in the writing of them.

Sometimes I'm asked 'Do you only write for children' or 'Do you do any real writing?' Isaac Singer came up with a memorable reply to these questions:

> Children are the best readers of genuine literature. Grown-ups are hypnotised by big names, exaggerated quotes and high-pressure advertising . . . The child is still the independent reader who relies on nothing but his own taste . . . Names and authorities mean nothing to him . . . No matter how young they are, children are deeply concerned with so-called eternal questions. Who created the world? Who made the earth, the sky, people, animals. Children cannot imagine the beginning or the end of time and space . . . Children think about and ponder such matters as justice, the purpose of life, the why of suffering. They often find it difficult to make peace with the idea that animals are slaughtered so that man can eat them. They are bewildered and frightened by death. They cannot accept that the strong should rule the weak.

Isaac Bashevis Singer
Are Children the Ultimate Literary Critics?

This is true and inspiring, even when it sometimes seems that brand-names are more important to children than justice or the why of suffering. I wish I could have written such a wise and uncompromising statement of belief.

Stuart Paterson